LEARNING TO STEP TOGETHER
Building and Strengthening Stepfamilies

A handbook for step-parents and parents

**Adapted and revised by Tim Kahn
With acknowledgement to
Cecile Currier and
the Stepfamily Association of America**

© National Stepfamily Association

ISBN 1 873309 17 1

Edited by Erica De'Ath STEPFAMILY
Printed by Nuffield Press
Design and layout by Claire George, STEPFAMILY

About the author:
Tim Kahn has worked in the field of parent education and
support for the last ten years. He contributes to national
magazines and newspapers and works as a consultant for
radio and television. He is involved with a number of parent
support organisations.

Acknowledgements

This book was produced as part of a pack to help those who wanted to provide or be part of a group for step-parents and parents.

In 1993 we asked our members to help produce some training materials for us in small and large workshop groups and discussion groups. The messages were unanimous - we need two items. A group facilitators guide and a handbook for step-parents and parents to help prepare, build and strengthen stepfamilies both for the children and the adults.

In 1994 we approached Marks and Spencers for financial support and were then able to commission Tim Kahn, already well-known for his work with Parent Network, to produce a step by step facilitator's guide based on a manual for group leaders produced by Cecile Currier for the Stepfamily Association of America.

The separate facilitators guide sets out the details for running an eight week course of two hour sessions.

Special thanks are due to:
- the original adapters of the SAA materials - Donna Smith and Jane Batchelor
- for the production of the first manuscript - Carol Harris
- to over 60 members of STEPFAMILY who participated in small and large group sessions and those who facilitated the groups
- many others who have read and used the materials and provided valuable comments

- the author Tim Kahn who took on board so many different people's comments
- the Community Affairs Department of Marks and Spencer whose financial support finally made this publication possible.

Erica De'Ath   November 1995

Contents

Introduction

"Julie was such an adorable well-behaved little girl, I just thought I would be able to deal with her the same as my own daughter."

"It never occurred to us that two seven year old boys that didn't really know each other would object to sharing a bedroom. They were both our sons and foolishly we thought they would be like twin-brothers."

Many people begin stepfamily life with the belief that it will be the same as life in a first family. When they join a stepfamily they discover, often painfully, that it is not. Complex challenges face those of us involved in stepfamilies, particularly as there are few guidelines to help us work out how to live in our stepfamily. Challenges such as:

♦ how do I show my stepchildren that I love them as well as my birth children?

♦ how do I deal with my stepchild's anger at and rejection of me?

♦ how do my new partner and I handle discipline in the family?

This book is designed to be part of a course 'Learning to Step Together' designed to help you - parents and step-parents involved in stepfamilies, or people working with stepfamilies - explore many of the issues that will help you successfully understand and manage stepfamily life. However, if you can't attend a group this book will give you valuable insights into stepfamily life.

You will find 'Learning to Step Together' helpful:

+ whether you are a birth parent or a step-parent,
+ whether you are just about to embark on life in a stepfamily,
+ whether you are living in your stepfamily or whether you are living apart from the stepfamily where your children live or,
+ whether you just want to have a better understanding of how stepfamilies work.

This series of sessions and handbook will introduce new ways of looking at relationships in stepfamilies that are special and unique.

You are likely to find it particularly useful if your partner is involved in this with you. Some couples are able to attend a group together but practical issues (such as childcare) often pose a problem. You may be attending this group without your partner. In this case we would encourage you to share what you are learning in the group with your partner: talk about the issues that you have discussed in the group (bearing in mind the agreement about confidentiality) and invite your partner to read the Handbook with you. Your partner may wish to join a future 'Learning to Step Together' group so that you can both share more fully in the experience of building and strengthening your stepfamily.

These notes are for you to use at home. They have been divided into sections with the same titles as the sessions in the course and are intended for you to use as back-up material after you have attended each session. The notes go over the areas you covered in the session and include additional ideas and information on the topics.

We have suggested a few activities for you to do (either on your own or with members of your family). We would encourage you to do them as they may help you understand or see an aspect of your family in a new light. And at the end of each section there is a blank page for you to write any thoughts, insights or feelings you have had, either while taking the course or while reading the notes.

If you find it a struggle to read the notes, then feel free to dip into them as and when you have the chance, or put them aside and read them at a later date. You are sure to get lots of ideas from just participating in 'Learning to Step Together' and the Handbook is there for you when you feel able to use it.

Language and terminology

Finding the words to differentiate between parent and step-parent, and to describe the complexity of stepfamily relationships is hard. In this Handbook we have chosen to use the term birth parent in preference to biological or natural parent. We use the term stepfamily to describe households in which children live with a parent and step-parent, as well as those with a parent and step-parent whom children visit or stay with, for example at weekends or holidays. Thus the term step-parent is used to describe those whose stepchildren do not live with them, as well as those who are in a full-time step-parenting role.

Ongoing support

If you are reading this because you are part of a 'Learning to Step Together' group, when you have come to the end of the course some, or all, of the members of your group may wish to continue meeting. Your group leader will discuss with you whether you would like to continue and if so, how you would like to organise it.

'Learning to Step Together' is just a beginning. You will gain new understandings of stepfamily life and the course will introduce you to new skills that will help your relationships with the members of your stepfamily (and probably anybody else you come into contact with).

However, it can be difficult to keep these ideas in mind and continue practising the skills without the support of others who are thinking and acting along similar lines. This is why we encourage you to continue meeting with others from your group. Not only are you likely to enjoy the contact with a group of people you have grown close to over the duration of the course, but you will find the meetings and discussions beneficial too.

Your group may like to continue meeting monthly - or in some other pattern. You may like to repeat some of the material that was covered in the first eight sessions, to choose additional topics to focus on or just to meet socially with others living in step. Your group leader will allow time in the final session for you to discuss this issue and fix a date for a next meeting if that is what your group decides to do.

Your group leader may be willing to continue to be involved with the group either as a participant or in a consultative role, advising you on how to get started and getting yourselves established - if that would be useful to you.

In addition to help from your group leader in setting up ongoing support, you may wish to contact the National STEPFAMILY Association for a copy of their Group Starter

Pack. The STEPFAMILY Helpline is always available for advice and support. You may also be able to get support from local organisations such as Home-Start, Parentline, Parent Network or a local family centre.

Good luck on your journey.

1
What is a stepfamily?

"She's more like a big friend than a Mum. She's just someone who lives with my Dad and who looks after me when I visit him."

"My real home is with my Mum, and Tom, my Stepdad, and my brothers and stepsisters and our new baby and the dog. In my other home I have a cat and two babies and a Stepmum called Liz."

"I've got two stepfamilies. I'm really pleased my Mum and Dad have both settled down again and each has a new family. But sometimes I feel I don't really belong in either."

Stepfamilies: myths and realities

To understand our stepfamily, we need to define what a stepfamily is.

First marriage families have been called 'nuclear, biological, real, natural, or intact' families. Stepfamilies have been referred to as 'reorganised, reconstituted, blended, reordered, combined, or remarried' families.

Comparing terms for first marriage families and stepfamilies often gives us the feeling that there is something 'second best' about stepfamilies. And, for many, it is inappropriate as it is a first marriage for one partner even if it is a remarriage for the other. This feeling often contributes to a sense of isolation, since many people don't want to openly identify themselves as belonging to a stepfamily. However, we know that there are many different types of families where children and adults can find personal growth, satisfaction and happiness. Certainly a stepfamily is one of these.

A stepfamily can be described as a family in which there is an adult couple in the household with at least one of the adults having a child from a previous relationship. This broad definition includes families in which children live with one parent and a step-parent, and families in which children from a previous relationship visit their parent and step-parent.

Step-parents are often labelled as 'non-parents, half parents, acquired parents, added parents, second parents, and part-time' parents. The term step-parent is old and myth-ridden. The word comes from an Old English word 'steop' meaning orphaned. This term came into popular usage when many children who had stepmothers had been orphaned because of the early death of their birth mother. Today most children become stepchildren as a result of parental divorce or separation. Stepfamilies are an increasingly common family form.

Over one in three marriages currently entered into in the UK ends in divorce. Over half of the divorces involve dependant children, around 450 children under 16 every day. Many people go on to remarry or live with a new partner, and so create a stepfamily. It is estimated that by the year 2000 there are likely to be between 2.5 and 3 million children and young people in stepfamilies in the UK. In 1991 there were already over one million children under 16 living in a stepfamily and a similar number who were members of a part-time stepfamily.

Different forms of stepfamilies

As a member of a stepfamily you will be aware that your family is different from a nuclear family. However, you may not be aware that much of the stress you feel in your life comes from the unique structure of your stepfamily as well as the normal patterns of stepfamily life. What is that unique but normal structure?

First, stepfamilies are born of loss; the loss of a partner through death, divorce or separation. The dream that you would settle down, have children and live happily ever after has been shattered. For adults not previously married, the loss of the fantasy of what his or her marriage would be like; and for the children, loss or a partial loss of a parental relationship.

Since stepfamilies are born of loss, there are many old loyalties that make the stepfamily structure complex and challenging. Stepfamily life involves children in a web of extra relationships, pulling and tugging at the family's emotions and security as they struggle to establish their own identity.

Often in their effort to fit into society, stepfamilies try to present themselves as nuclear families. While all families today face pressures, the extremely complex set of relationships, old loyalties and differing value systems surrounding the stepfamily creates extra stresses for its members. Stepfamilies often outwardly resemble a nuclear family. People assume that the roles, the rules, and the relationships within a stepfamily also resemble those of a nuclear family. We know that this is not the case.

The expectation that stepfamilies and nuclear families are the same puts great pressure on stepfamily members. It is helpful to be aware of the structure of stepfamilies and to understand how their characteristics differ from those of the nuclear family and have an impact on the relationships that exist within stepfamilies.

> Remember that many of the common difficulties of family life also occur in stepfamilies and can be magnified by the unique structure of stepfamilies.

Stepfamily members have previously established roles, values, and lifestyles when they come together. Often their values about food, discipline, money, privacy and many other issues are different. These feelings can cause confusion, conflict and hurt feelings in stepfamilies when there is little preparation for blending different lifestyles in one household.

It is important in stepfamilies to learn to recognise and tolerate differences in feelings and attitudes. For the stepfamily, the areas of disagreement are usually more numerous than in a nuclear family, and the attendant feelings are more intense because of prior histories and loyalties. A father may consider his children well-behaved while a stepmother considers them rude and unappreciative. One of the parents may have raised the children with corporal punishment, while the other has raised the children with reasoning and discussion as a means of discipline. The tolerance to differences is very crucial to successful stepfamily life.

How stepfamilies differ from birth families

♦ All individuals have suffered important losses: relationships, dreams of what their marriage and family would be like.

♦ All individuals in the family come together with previous family histories.

♦ Parent-child relationships were formed before the new couple relationship.

♦ There is a birth parent elsewhere in actuality, or in memory, with power and influence over family members.

♦ Children are members of two households if they have contact with both birth parents.

♦ Little legal relationship exists between step-parents and stepchildren.

Issues that can cause conflict in stepfamilies

1. The feelings, values and lifestyles of each family member existed prior to becoming a stepfamily. The demand to deal on a daily basis with different styles of living can create tremendous pressure.

2. Relationships between children and their birth parent existed prior to the new couple relationship. Many times there are special bonds that develop in the single-parent home during the transition from separation to stepfamily. Often the bonds between the parent and the children are extremely close, and it takes time for a step-parent to be accepted. The step-parent may feel like an outsider, and children may resent the intrusion of another adult into their lives.

3. A birth parent may live elsewhere and have great influence on family members. This absent parent can exert a tremendous emotional force on the family by

appearing to compete with or criticise the other parent and/or step-parent. Stepfamilies may often feel helpless when the non-residential parent involves themselves in the organisation of their household, holiday plans or family budget. This may be particularly so over child support, whether it is coming into or going out of the stepfamily.

4. Children are often members of two households. This means that the children are affected by a process of adjustment and re-adjustment as they visit their mother's or father's home. Children often feel confusion and conflict at first about the different rules and standards that may exist in the two homes. They can experience loyalty conflicts (such as "Who should I like more?"), and may feel torn between their birth parents. The role of the visiting child may be ambiguous to the adults and the children. Are they considered to be full family members or visitors? The lack of clear role expectations may confuse the child, and so cause unpredictable behaviour.

5. The role of step-parents is poorly defined in our society. There are times when a step-parent is called upon to act as a parent, and other times as a friend. Neither step-parents nor other family members may really know what is realistic and workable to expect from step-parents. Often parents and step-parents try a succession of roles not really feeling comfortable in any.

6. There is still a limited legal relationship between a step-parent and a stepchild. The 1989 Children Act permits step-parents to apply for a residence or contact order and to acquire parental responsibility. However it still does

not place the step-parent on a par with a parent since it does not give the right to make major decisions about guardianship or adoption and is usually only effective until the child reaches 16 years old.

7. Step-relationships are new and constantly being tested. The new partners choose each other. However, the children have to relate to a step-parent and possibly stepsiblings for whom they have no particular warm feelings or connection. Simultaneously, children may feel pushed out by the new couple relationship. There is no shared family history.

8. Stepfamilies take on a whole new set of relations who may put pressure on them to exclude prior extended family members. This can cause particular difficulties for grandparents who want to keep in touch, and step-grandparents who feel no need to establish links with step-grandchildren unknown to them.

Stepfamilies and myths

Exercise: stepfamily tree
   In addition to the structural characteristics of stepfamilies and the differing values and feelings, the large number of people involved in their stepfamily can seem overwhelming. See the sample family tree in the stepfamily forest opposite.

   Fill in your own stepfamily tree. You may be surprised at how many people you are now related to.

A Stepfamily Forest from STEPFAMILIES, New Patterns of Harmony *by Linda Craven*

19

Myths

There are many cultural myths that also challenge the stepfamily. Five major myths appear to create the most common difficulties for stepfamily life.

1. *"Stepfamilies are the same as nuclear families."*
   This myth establishes unrealistic expectations for stepfamilies and often creates rules and role expectations that are not workable. Stepfamilies are different from nuclear families and so work in a different way.

2. *"The death of a partner makes step-parenting easier."*
   In fact, often the death of a partner makes step-parenting harder because it is difficult to compete with an idealised image of a dead parent. Surviving children may place their dead parent on a pedestal and see them as perfect. As a consequence, the step-parent can be condemned for their apparent deficiencies and never really be accepted.

3. *"Stepchildren are easier to manage when they are not living in the home."*
   Often this is not the case. When stepchildren visit, it can be difficult to establish a routine and basic rules. When stepchildren live in the home, it is possible to establish daily routines and expectations that may help adjustment.

4. *"Love happens instantly."*
   This is probably the most difficult and destructive myth, particularly for stepmothers. Many stepmothers feel that they should love and care for their stepchildren as if they were their own. This is impossible, as love takes time to develop and grow. This myth sets up many expectations that will hamper stepfamily adjustment. Stepmothers may feel guilty and unhappy when they are not able to

meet their own or their partner's expectation that they will love their stepchildren. This can lead to anger and disappointment for the couple, and resentment towards the stepchildren.

5. *"Stepchildren settle better if their separated parent withdraws."*
   Children who appear to make the best adjustment are not those who are cut off from a parent, but rather, those who are able to have a continuing relationship with both parents, plus step-parents, in an atmosphere of co-operation. This can be difficult to establish and maintain.

Appreciating our stepchildren and children - and ourselves

We all know how good it feels when somebody tells us what they like about us or something we have done. It makes us feel good inside. And we also know instinctively how important it is to appreciate our stepchildren and children and encourage them in their efforts. Yet, despite this, many of us seem compelled to point out our stepchildren and children's mistakes and tell them what they are doing wrong. At the same time we often neglect to tell our stepchildren and children what we like about them and the things they do. That leaves our stepchildren and children feeling discouraged.

The compulsion to point out our stepchildren and children's mistakes may arise from our fear that if we don't, they will never learn from them. But, as in the case of Jenny and Susan (see box below), such actions have the opposite effect from that intended. We may also feel we should limit the amount of appreciation we give to our children so that they don't get big-headed. But most 'big-heads' suffer from a lack of confidence born out of a lack of appreciation and encouragement. They cover it up by acting 'big'.

> Jenny remembers constant criticism from her parents. *"They had the best of intentions. They pointed out my mistakes so that I could learn from them. But I ended up feeling I was no good. And so I promised myself I would be different with my own children.*
>
> *"I now make a point of telling my stepdaughter, Susan, what I like about her and what she does. It seems to help her feel good and I'm sure she feels stronger in herself than I did when I was a child"*

It can make a crucial difference for our stepchildren and children if we appreciate them and tell them what we like about what they do. And putting our attention on the positive tends to reinforce the positive.

We all need to know that we are liked and loved by the people who are close to us. Saying "I like being with you" can mean so much to a child. Our stepchildren and children need encouragement when they are learning new skills. We can, for instance, say: "Well done for persevering. After a lot of struggle you have learnt..." When our stepchildren and children know that they have our complete support, they feel empowered to face the challenges of daily life.

Exercise:

Make a list of (at least) ten things that you like about each of your children and stepchildren. These may include their qualities and things that they do. Find a time to tell each of them at least one of those things, and choose something that you have never told them before. Notice the effect this has on them.

What I Like About	
Name of Child	Name of Child
1 2 3 4 5 6 7 8 9 10	1 2 3 4 5 6 7 8 9 10
Name of Child	Name of Child
1 2 3 4 5 6 7 8 9 10	1 2 3 4 5 6 7 8 9 10

And just as we appreciate our stepchildren and children, so we can also appreciate ourselves. It may sound easy but so many of us notice our own 'failings' and constantly run ourselves down inside our heads. As we learn to put our attention on what we do well, we feel better and achieve more through our increased sense of self-worth.

Make a list of (at least) ten things that you like about yourself. Remind yourself of those things, particularly at times when you are feeling low.

Ten Things I Like About me	
1	6
2	7
3	8
4	9
5	10

Summary

Stepfamilies are different but no less important or valuable than other types of families. Stepfamilies present many challenges to all their members to achieve satisfaction and positive experiences.

The more we understand some of the issues and concerns that occur in all stepfamilies the easier it may be to accept ourselves, our children and stepchildren for what we are and to appreciate each other.

Notes to myself on what I have learned

2
The new stepfamily

"After so many years on my own it was wonderful to have someone to turn to, not just to discuss money and other worries, but more to be able to look back on the day and enjoy it with another person."

" My children were really worried about me being lonely and on my own but at the same time they didn't want to share me with anyone new."

Expectations and the couple relationship

There are several reasons why it is important to think about the expectations for stepfamily life. First, many couples enter the new relationship with different yet vague ideas about what they want for each other. Unclear expectations and hidden agendas can cause resentments and emotional distance in a stepfamily couple. It is helpful if expectations are made explicit so each of you can understand what the other person hopes for and wants.

For a couple's relationship in a stepfamily to be strong, it is important that each person can be open about what they expect and hope for from family life. The couple relationship in a stepfamily is the key relationship, just as it is in a nuclear family. The strength of the relationship between the couple affects the entire family. The parents are models providing direction and leadership for the family. Since the stresses in stepfamilies can be more intense than they are in a nuclear family, it makes sense that the stepcouple's relationship is even more important, and needs to be strong and mutually supportive. It is essential that couples make their relationship a top priority.

A parent may put more emotional energy towards their children than towards their partner, especially after a period of single parenting. It helps to remember that adult-adult relationships and parent-child relationships are different in quality from one another and therefore need not be competing relationships.

Often stepcouples have dreams for their stepfamily that would be more appropriate in a nuclear family. They may want the children to love their partner as they do, or they may want the partner to have strong feelings for their children. When they find that these hopes do not materialise, they may experience disappointment and resentment. Since the stepfamily structure is unique, it is helpful if stepcouples find special and different ways to relate to one another and develop closeness. These approaches need not be modelled on nuclear family norms.

The goal is not to become a nuclear family, but for you each to develop a family style that is right for you, that provides the nurturing and the security that all of the members in your stepfamily need.

Topics to discuss with children

It is helpful if the birth parents have already talked about the divorce, separation or death with their children. Even if this has been discussed earlier, it often comes up at the time of the stepfamily formation and needs to be dealt with again. The following guidelines touch on major areas of concern for children.

1. **Confirm the parent's relationship has ended as a couple.**
   If parents have divorced or separated, give the children concrete reasons why their parents relationship ended, and why reconciliation is impossible, for example "We were very unhappy living together", or "You may remember that your father and I were always arguing". Beware of assigning blame to any one person in the family. Be clear in your explanations, and be willing to repeat them. This is necessary because children often ask why parents don't reconcile and become a 'family' again 'the way it used to be'.

2. **Confirm the children were not responsible.**
   Point out that the children were not responsible for the separation and that they did not cause it; nor can they bring their parents back together again.

3. **Confirm the children are still loved.**
   Reassure the children that they are still loved and cared for by their birth parents. This may need to be repeated several times because many children find the idea difficult to believe and accept. However, if one parent is not involved with the children or showing concern for the children, help the children express their feelings about this. Accept their sadness and anger about the lack of contact, but don't make excuses for the other parent. Talking together can help.

4. **Confirm the value of the separated parent.**
   It is helpful if the children can maintain good feelings toward both parents. Try not to blame or 'rubbish' the other parent to the children, as children find this very distressing. A co-operative relationship between birth

parents will enhance the child's ability to accept a step-parent.

5. **Confirm both parents will remain parents.**
Ideally, both birth parents can remain involved with the children and continue to parent in a joint or shared way.

It is also helpful for the child to have consistent contact with each birth parent. Children may need reassurance from both parents that they will continue to be loved, and that neither parent is going to stop being a parent because they are no longer together. If the children feel secure that there will be an on-going relationship with both parents, they will be more able to accept a step-parent and will be more comfortable in developing a relationship with their step-parent.

6. **Confirm it is OK to talk about death.**
For a child whose parent has died it is also important to explain how they died and to answer any questions as honestly and age-appropriately as possible. Our society has a taboo around talking about death and we often exclude children from the experience of death with the aim of protecting them from the pain. However, this only serves to confuse children and they need the space to ask and talk about the death of the parent and feel and express whatever feelings they have about it.

7. **Confirm it is OK to have feelings.**
The birth parents need to allow the children the opportunity to express emotions of anger, sadness and fear that they may have about the ending of their parents' relationship and any feelings they may have about either parent's new relationship. Even though this can be

difficult to do, parents need to listen to these feelings and assure the children that they will continue to be available to them to discuss their concerns.

8. **Confirm practical arrangements.**
Explain to the children some basic facts (such as where they will live, who will take care of them, when they will see their other parent, and any matters such as changing schools) at the time of the separation, again at divorce and especially when a new partner is joining the family. Children need the reassurance of knowing - and that may mean telling them nothing is changing (e.g. no new home or school, or change in care or contact).

9. **Confirm consistency, limit changes.**
Try to maintain some consistency in the children's lives. If possible, avoid simultaneous changes such as moving, changing schools, or changing babysitters. Often this cannot be avoided. If abrupt changes are unavoidable, it is helpful if children are forewarned and that each change is discussed with them.

Explain that you would have preferred it not to be this way and acknowledge that they may be cross and find the situation difficult. Tell them that you will try and minimise the stress for them in what is bound to be a difficult time.

Topics to discuss as a stepcouple
Before couples create their stepfamilies or shortly thereafter, it is helpful to talk together at some length about important changes. The following suggestions touch on some of the areas of concern:

Things to talk about before forming a stepfamily .....
.... or shortly afterwards

1. Reasons for remarrying or living together:
   * What is it that you really want from this relationship?

2. Changes that living together will bring:
   * How are your lifestyles different?
   * What are the similarities and differences in your beliefs about child rearing, family rules, housekeeping, food and money?
   * How do you feel about moving into a home where your partner has lived with a former partner?

3. How will remarriage or cohabitation affect your children?
   * What effect will it have on your children's relationship with the other parent?

4. What does the step-parent expect and want from his or her stepchildren.
   * What does he or she expect and want from his or her own children?

5. How will you communicate with former partners?
   * How much contact is appropriate?
   * Will you be able to accommodate visiting stepchildren and give them their own space or room?

6. How will money be handled?
   * Are you aware of each other's assets and debts?
   * How will maintenance and child support payments affect your family budget?

7. What are your feelings about religion in your home,

about contact with your extended family, and your general value system?

8. How will you make time for yourself to enjoy your new couple relationship?

9. What will your stepchildren call you?

10. How will household responsibilities be shared?
    * What kind of parenting is expected of you and what do you expect of your partner?

11. Will you each discipline your own children?
    * When will you think it appropriate to discipline stepchildren?
    * How will you both explain your policy to all the children?

It is important to be open and honest with each other in a positive way.
Compare the similarities and the differences in your beliefs about child rearing and discipline. Talk about where you are going to live and how you are going to feel about it (for example, moving into the house where an ex-partner has lived). Talk about some of the issues related to territory, 'ghosts', and financial considerations (such as, how space will be shared, privacy, possessions from a former partner that may be part of your current home, how maintenance and child support payments will be used).

Talk with your children about the changes forming a stepfamily will bring:
* new living arrangements,

- new family relationships, stepsiblings, and
- less time for you and the children.

Also discuss the effects that this will have on their relationship with their other parent. Ask them what they hope for in the stepfamily.

Encourage your children to spend ample time with your future partner.
It is best if they can get to know each other and feel comfortable with each other before the idea of living together is introduced to them. It can be important for step-parents to have some time alone with each stepchild, to promote the growth of these new relationships, when they feel comfortable being with each other.

Discuss with your new partner issues related to dealing with ex-partners.
- What will the rules of etiquette be?
- How much contact will there be and around what issues will contact be made?
- How will you handle it if an ex-partner is overly friendly, is used to dropping in unexpectedly, or is sabotaging contact or access visits or the new couple relationship?

We have listed some tips on communicating with ex-partners on page 36.

This can be a very emotional and problematic area of stepfamily life. Many couples have used certain approaches for keeping former partner relationships on a businesslike basis (see box of tips).

Discuss family finances with your new partner.
An open and honest survey of your assets and debts may
reduce any kind of unrealistic expectations and ensuing
resentments that may result. Discuss maintenance and child
support payments that must be made and those that will be
received. What impact will this have on your budget. (See
pages 142-146.)

Talk about beliefs and values in general such as,
religion, politics and moral issues.
It is important to share your beliefs about your childrearing
practices, your extended families, and your religious
expectations with each other. It helps to listen to each other
carefully, and to accept that differences are not bad or good,
they are to be expected and can enhance a relationship.

Discuss how you are going to find time for yourself
and for the two of you.
It's actually very important, especially if the children live with
you, that you have time alone to develop and enjoy your
couple relationship. Because you are an 'instant' family,
individual needs and couples' needs must be planned for, to
ensure time for yourselves.

Discuss with your stepchildren what they will call you.
It is generally most comfortable if you let the children decide
what they want to call their new step-parent. This
arrangement seems to work best. Their choices may change
over time.

Discuss how tasks and household responsibilities will
be shared between the two of you.
Who is expected to take care of the shopping and the

cooking? Who is expected to pay the bills and take care of the garden? What kind of parenting is expected from each of you? Discuss very specifically how these tasks will be divided and how you feel about such matters.

It is valuable to discuss these issues well in advance of forming your stepfamily and to discuss them several times. If you are currently living together and have not discussed some of these things with your partner, it could be helpful to take the time this week to do so. It is important that each topic be dealt with separately. Try to be candid and open with the other about your feelings and expectations. You may find that you can best discuss these difficulties together with some assistance. Remember that you cannot always control the ways in which ex-partners may interfere with your stepfamily life, so sharing feelings about this interference may reduce some of the resentment.

All the topics listed above have an impact on any family. The major difference in stepfamilies is that you are an 'instant' family, and have tremendous pressures to parent, divide financial resources, and develop couple intimacy all at the same time. The demands of being a new partner and a parent simultaneously place great strain on many stepfamilies, often exhausting the couple who immediately try to fill both the role of parent and partner. Therefore, candid discussion, or openness, increases the chances of avoiding resentment and helps in having clear expectations of each other. If there is agreement between you on many of these issues, getting through the initial phases of development of your stepfamily will be smoother.

Tips on communicating with an ex-partner

1. Arrange times to talk about the children, by phone or by meeting, rather than hurried exchanges on the doorstep.

2. Keep conversation focused on arranging visits, children's issues (medical, dental, school) and financial matters.

3. Share information about your child, so you both can appreciate his or her unique characteristics.

4. Discourage personal talk about topics such as the intimate details of each other's personal lives.

5. Use 'I' statements and not 'You' statements, we discuss this on pages 67-69 in the section entitled 'Owning our feelings'.

6. Do not relay messages to ex-partners through children.

7. Keep to commitments about visiting, contact, maintenance and child support payments as closely as possible.

8. If communication through verbal means is impossible, try written communication.

9. Do not give in to inappropriate demands from ex-partners, such as fixing the plumbing, working on the car or frequent last minute changes in contact or access visits.

10. If the former partner is sabotaging contact or access visits, focus on the children's needs and how this behaviour effects the children's well-being, using clear messages.

11. If you are too angry to negotiate, find someone to help you discuss unresolved issues. Maybe a counsellor, therapist or minister could mediate or provide post-divorce counselling to enable you and your ex-partner to negotiate.

Acknowledging our children's feelings

Our children share their feelings at every moment. Those feelings may include excitement at a new discovery, frustration at shoelaces that won't tie, laughter and joy in a game you are playing together, tears when a favourite toy is lost or tantrums when they can't have one more biscuit.

Children start to control their feelings when they learn that it is not the done thing to show them, or they start to hide their feelings when they do not feel there is space for them to be expressed. Some examples of particular situations in which this can occur in stepfamilies are listed below:

♦ They may feel that their angry or sad feelings are destructive and may hurt others in the family whom they love.

♦ They may see their parent or parents being overwhelmed by their own feelings and sense that there is nobody to listen to their feelings.

♦ They may not recognise their own feelings and act them out in a destructive way. For example, a child who is angry that their parent died or left, may take out their rage at their new step-parent.

♦ They may feel that being friendly to their step-parent means they are being disloyal to their absent parent. Thus they may act 'cool' towards their step-parent when in fact they actually have warm feelings towards them.

You will feel comfortable with many of your children's feelings and they will intuitively sense your ease. However, you may feel uncomfortable with other feelings and you may inadvertently try to find ways of stopping your children from expressing them.

You may find your children's sadness difficult. When they cry about the absence of their parent (your ex-partner) you may notice yourself quickly changing the subject because it is too painful for you to see their sadness, and perhaps you feel guilty for having 'caused' that sadness.

Maybe you find their anger difficult for similar reasons. You may respond to any outbursts of anger with harshness "Don't talk about your mother/father like that", or maybe you say quietly: "We don't get angry in this house". Or maybe you just have a painful look on your face. However you communicate it, your children will intuitively learn that certain feelings are unacceptable. They may stop expressing those feelings in order to avoid your reaction or they may feel compelled to express them over and over again in a vain attempt to try and understand your reaction.

Acknowledging your children's feelings helps them learn that *all* feelings are acceptable. A father talked about his seven-year old son: "Jamie really misses his mother. He often cries in his bed because he misses her bedtime stories and goodnight kisses. I usually talk with him about his mother and show him that I understand his sadness. And my wife, his stepmother, is learning to do the same. It's not so easy for her because she can easily feel 'second-best' at such times. But we both recognise how important it is for him to know that we accept and understand the way he feels."

The more children are allowed to express their painful feelings and to have those feelings accepted and acknowledged by the people around them, the sooner those feelings are likely to go away - and the same is true for adults too.

> Remember: If a child is not allowed to express their painful feelings those feelings can lie buried for a long time and are likely to trouble them at a later date without them knowing what is actually bothering them.

When our stepchildren or children are raging with anger, or when they are tearful and upset, we may feel the urge to say: "Don't make such a fuss", or "Be quiet, I can't stand that noise". Hearing our children express their painful feelings often reminds us unconsciously of childhood pain that we may not have been allowed to express. That then makes it hard to listen to our stepchildren or children letting out theirs. However, taking the time to acknowledge your stepchildren's or children's feelings will help them heal from the pain that is causing the outburst.

In some cases the acknowledgement will seem to work like magic. Your stepchild or child will feel understood and the upset will pass immediately. In many cases, however, your stepchild or child may continue to be upset and your acknowledgement may actually invite further outbursts of upset as they sense that they can really show the depth of their pain because you seem to understand. In either case, your acknowledgement will help your stepchild or child deal with the painful feelings that are troubling them.

The more your children can express painful feelings about a particular subject, the more those feelings will be reduced, so that they will overwhelm the child less and less as time goes by.

While being accepting and understanding of our stepchildren's or children's feelings, there are times when we need to contain the way they express them. Feelings are always acceptable, it's just the way of expressing them that may be unacceptable.

We can show our stepchildren and children that we still love them *with* their angry feelings, while at the same time channelling the expression of their feelings into an acceptable outlet. If one sibling is angry with another, we might hold a younger child firmly and lovingly while saying: "I can see that you are very angry with your brother and I will not let you hurt him. You can show me how angry you are". The child may scream and shout and cry and hit out in the safety of our arms until the angry feelings are through. In this way the angry child will be able to let out their feelings without hurting the other. We can encourage our stepchildren and children to express their painful feelings while setting a framework which prevents them from damaging themselves, other people, or our possessions.

Punishing children for their 'bad' feelings does not help them. It makes them feel bad about themselves and pushes the feelings underground until the next outburst. When children are caught up in the grip of strong emotions, it is as if they have been taken over by a monster. At such times they are no longer in control of themselves and they need us to provide secure boundaries for them so that they can let the feelings out without doing any damage to themselves or others. This is not always easy, especially if their behaviour sparks off *our* angry and upset feelings which were squashed when we were young. Yet with practice we can learn it.

The healing power of tears

Many of us try to hush the tears of someone who is upset in the mistaken belief that the pain is in the tears rather than in the details of the upsetting event that happened. If our partner or one of our children or stepchildren is crying when thinking about or retelling the details of a painful event, we can most usefully stay with them and encourage them in the telling of the story while their tears continue to flow.

There is scientific evidence to show that stress is released when emotional tears are cried. But if we were discouraged from crying when we were young, then we often have an almost automatic reaction to discourage the tears in those who are upset around us. The more we can learn to express our sadness and allow our own tears to flow, the more easily we will be able to listen to the tears of others.

Acknowledging our own feelings

Acknowledging - and expressing - our own feelings goes hand in hand with acknowledging our stepchildren's and children's feelings. Mothers in particular often feel that their role is to sacrifice themselves and their needs for their children, so they get into the habit of putting their own feelings aside. Fathers were often told as boys that it is unmanly to show vulnerable feelings. As a result such feelings are often locked away inside them to such an extent that they don't even know they are there. As we lose touch with our own feelings, so we also lose touch with other people's feelings.

Acknowledging our feelings, even just saying "I feel fed up" or "I'm feeling great", can help us feel better in ourselves and shows our stepchildren and children by example that feelings are acceptable.

Summary

In stepfamilies, as in nuclear families, the couple relationship is of prime importance. One way of building and strengthening this relationship is by sharing expectations before creating the stepfamily and at intervals after its formation.

After a divorce, or loss of a parent through death or separation, children usually feel angry and confused. They need reasurrance and specific information about what changes will take place in their lives.

Notes to myself on what I have learned

3

Parents and step-parents

*"I knew I was in love with Bill and if it had been just
the two of us I'd have had no hesitation. But I kept
worrying about the kids. What if it didn't work out? I
couldn't bear to put them through all that distress
again."*

*"I just didn't know what to do for the best. Jimmie was
only five and he really wanted a man around the house
to play football and things with him. But Gemma who
was 13 was so jealous and angry it used to frighten
me."*

Stepfamily phases of development

The stepfamily has its own phases of development just as the
nuclear family does. In the nuclear family this would be:
marriage, birth of children, children growing up, the actual
departure of the children, and adjusting to being a couple
again.

The phases of development in a stepfamily can come in any
order and can be in a different order for different people.
They are:

1. Recovering from the loss of the old relationship.

2. Entering the new relationship and planning the new
   stepfamily.

3. Forming the stepfamily.

Phase one: accept the past

+ Relinquish and mourn the previous couple relationship. Feelings about these relationships need to be discussed and resolved over time. The depression, sadness and guilt that often accompany a death, a divorce or a separation, can hinder the development of the new couple relationship.

+ Help the children talk about any feelings of loss, sadness, jealousy and guilt that they may feel when they lose some of their time with you or with their other parent.

Phase two: plan for the future

+ Identify ways in which you have changed your attitudes and behaviours that will make this relationship different from the previous one.

+ Talk with your partner about any lack of self-confidence you may have regarding your ability to sustain relationships.

+ Be aware of the fear of repeating mistakes and the resulting insecurities and doubts regarding second relationships.

+ Accept the loss of the former family system, including letting go of the dream of the nuclear family, and giving up fantasies that you will recreate this in your stepfamily. This means giving up games with an ex-partner, giving up that intimate connection, negative or positive, and investing your emotional energies in the current relationship. If this happens, then the stepfamily can be a productive and satisfying family, even though its form is different and complex.

Phase three: restructure the family roles

♦ The children and their parent need to accept their step-parent's right to have a part in establishing rules and standards for the family. Initially the step-parent needs to develop a relationship with their stepchildren before slowly taking on tasks of disciplining, although some couples find the best way for them is for the step-parent not to be involved in disciplining. Because of the previous parent-child relationship and bonds, children respond more positively in the early stages to discipline from their parent than from their step-parent.

♦ Rebuilding general boundaries is important. This involves establishing a strong couple unity and clearly defining the discipline and decision-making functions within the couple relationship. It also involves clearly differentiating the couple relationship from the parenting relationship; which means there needs to be a special time for the parent and children to spend time alone, just as there is time alone for the couple. This helps the children learn that there are differences between parent-child and couple relationships, and decreases the children's sense of competitiveness with the step-parent.

♦ Help the children to understand the relationship with their other birth parent. Their feelings of loyalty, jealously, abandonment, sadness and guilt, will inevitably be present at the time of formation of the new family. With help, and over time, those feelings can change. What is needed are discussions between the parent and step-parent, with the children and (where possible) with the other parent also.

Accomplishment of these three phases does not happen over-
night. Many stepfamilies find it takes a number of years
before they have satisfactorily achieved all of them. Nor will
the phases necessarily be accomplished in the order presented
here. The new partners will not always progress at the same
rate - for example, one partner may need more time than the
other to recover from the loss of a previous relationship.
Sometimes conciliation, post-divorce counselling,
bereavement counselling or family therapy is helpful, as many
couples experience considerable stress in accomplishing these
tasks.

Guidelines for stepfamilies

1. Finding space

It is difficult to have a new person or persons move into
your 'space', and it is difficult to be the 'new' person or
people joining a pre-existing group. For these reasons it
can help to cut down feelings involved with 'territory' if
stepfamilies can start out in a new home, but for many
this will not be a practical reality.

2. Nourishing the couple

Parent-child relationships have preceded the new couple
relationship. Because of this, many parents feel that it is
a betrayal of the earlier parent-child bond to form a
primary relationship with their new partner. A primary
couple relationship, however, is usually crucial for the
continuing existence of the stepfamily, and therefore is
very important for the children as well as the adults. A
strong adult bond can protect the children from another
family loss, and it can also provide the children with a
positive model for their own eventual couple
relationships. The adults often need to arrange time
alone to help nourish this important couple relationship.

3. Building step-relationships

Forming new relationships within the stepfamily can be important, particularly when the children are young. Activities involving different subgroups of the stepfamily can help such relationships grow. For example, a step-parent and stepchildren might share a hobby or go shopping together.

4. Protecting old relationships

Protecting relationships is also important and can help reduce any loss at sharing a parent with a step-parent. So it is helpful for a parent and children to have their own time together, separate from stepfamily activities.

5. Take it slowly

Caring relationships take time to evolve. The expectation of 'instant love' between step-parents and stepchildren can lead to many disappointments and difficulties. If the stepfamily relationships are allowed to develop as seems comfortable to the individuals involved, then caring between step-relatives has the opportunity to develop.

6. Stepfamilies are different

Stepfamilies are structurally and emotionally different from first families. Upset and sadness is experienced by the children and at times by the adults as they react to the loss of their nuclear families or to the loss of the dream of a perfect marriage. Acceptance that a stepfamily is a different type of family is important, as is the recognition that many upsetting behaviours result from these feelings of insecurity and loss.

7. A child has two parents

Because children are part of two parents, they nearly always have strong pulls towards both of them. These divided loyalties often make it difficult for children to relate comfortably to all the parental adults in their lives. Rejection of a step-parent, for example, may have nothing to do with the personal characteristics of the step-parent. In fact, warm and loving step-parents may create especially severe loyalty conflicts for the children.

8. Children can love others

As children and adults are able to accept the fact that children can care for more than two parental adults, then the children's loyalty conflicts can diminish and the new step-relationships improve. While it may be helpful to the children for the adults to acknowledge negative as well as positive feelings about ex-partners, children may be caught in loyalty conflicts and feel personally insecure if specific critical remarks are made continuously about their other parent.

9. No parental wars

Courteous relationships between ex-partners are important, although they can be difficult for many adults to maintain, is especially helpful to the children, if such a relationship can be worked out. In such instances, the children do not get caught in the middle between two hostile parents, there is less need for the children to take sides, and the children are better able to accept and utilise the positive elements in their living arrangements.

Direct contact between the adults can be helpful since it does not place the children in the sometimes powerful position of being message carriers between their parents. Although it may be strained, many ex-partners are able to talk about their children if they focus on their mutual concern for their children's welfare.

10. Creating a stepfamily way

Children, as well as adults, already have a family history. Suddenly these individuals come together in a stepfamily and their sets of 'givens' are questioned. Much is to be gained by coming together as a stepfamily unit to work out and develop new family patterns and traditions. Even when the individuals are able to recognise that patterns are not 'right' or 'wrong', it takes time and patience to work out satisfying new alternatives.

11. Being on the look out for differences

Values, our underlying approach to life and general ways of doing things, do not shift easily. Within a stepfamily, different value systems are very common because of different previous family histories, and tolerance for these differences can help smooth the process of stepfamily integration. Needs, specific ways individuals relate together, individual preferences, etc. can usually be negotiated more quickly than other general values. Being aware, and on the look-out for such difficulties can make for more flexibility and relaxation in the stepfamily unit. Negotiation and renegotiation is needed by most families.

12. Step-parent not parent

Being a step-parent is an unclear and sometimes difficult task. The wicked stepmother myth contributes to the discomfort of many women, and cultural, structural and personal factors affect the step-parent role. Partners can be very helpful to one another if they are able to be supportive with the working out of new family patterns. Step-parenting is usually more successful if step-parents carve out a role for themselves that is different from and does not compete with the birth parents.

13. Being clear about discipline

While discipline is not usually accepted by stepchildren until a friendly relationship has been established (often taking two or more years), both adults do need to support each other's authority in the household. The parent may be the primary disciplinarian initially, but when that person is unavailable, it is often necessary for the parent to give a clear message to the children that the step-parent is acting as an 'authority figure' for both adults in his or her absence.

14. Keeping punishments within the stepfamily

Unity between the couple is important to the functioning of the stepfamily. When partners are comfortable together, differences between them in regard to the children can sometimes be worked out in the presence of the children, but it helps neither children nor adults to let the children approach each adult separately and 'divide and conquer'. When disciplinary action is necessary keep it within the stepfamily household, otherwise many resentful feelings can be generated.

15. Moving on rather than settling in

Integrating a stepfamily that contains teenagers can be particularly difficult. At this age adolescents are moving away from their families in any type of family. In lone parent families teenagers have often been 'young adults', and with the creation of a stepfamily they find it extremely difficult or impossible to return to being in a 'child' position again.

Adolescents have more of a previous 'family history' and so they usually appreciate having considerable opportunity to be part of the stepfamily negotiations, although they may withdraw from both parents and not wish to be part of any or many of the 'stepfamily' activities.

16. More than a visitor

'Visiting' children may feel strange and are often outsiders in the neighbourhood. It can be helpful if they have some place in the household that is their own. For example, a drawer or a shelf for toys and clothes. If they are included in stepfamily chores and projects when they are with the stepfamily, they tend to feel more connected to the group. Bringing a friend with them to share the visit and having some active adult participation in becoming integrated into the neighbourhood can make a difference to many visiting children. Knowing ahead of time that there is going to be an interesting activity can sometimes give visiting children a sense of anticipation.

Parents and step-parents in the household that children visit are often concerned because they have so little time to transmit their values to the children. Children tend to resist concerted efforts by the adults to instil stepfamily ideals during each visit, and such efforts are often counter productive. It is comforting to parents and step-parents to learn that the examples of behaviour and relationship simply observed in the household are more likely to affect choices made by all the children as they grow up and enter adulthood.

17. Love, affection and sexuality

Sexuality is usually more apparent in stepfamilies because of the new couple relationship, and because children may suddenly be living with other children with whom they have not grown up. Also, there are not the usual incest taboos operating. It is important for the children to receive affection and to be aware of tenderness between the couple, but it may also be important for the couple to minimise to some extent the sexual aspects of the household, and to help the children understand and accept their sexual attractions to one another without acting on them.

18. Family stress is normal

All families experience stressful times. Children tend to show little day to day appreciation for their parents, and at times they get angry and reject them. Because stepfamilies are families born of loss, the mixture of feelings can be even more intense than in nuclear families. Jealously, rejection, guilt and anger can be more pronounced, and therefore expectations that the stepfamily will live 'happily ever after' is even more unrealistic than it is in first families. Being understanding and accepting of the many negative as well as positive feelings can result in less disappointment and more stepfamily enjoyment.

19. Keeping in touch is important

Keeping even minimal contact between adults and children can lead to future satisfaction since time and maturity bring many changes. With some communication between stepfamily members when children are young, satisfying interpersonal relationships often develop in the future when children become more independent in their relationships with both parents and with step-parents.

Pressures on parents

The wicked step-parent myth

There are several myths that shape our expectations about stepfamilies. Probably the most important one that stepfamilies live with is that love happens instantly. Studies show that fantasies and hopes for the perfect family play a larger role in stepfamilies than in nuclear families. Step-parents are ready to be rescuers and saviours, showering the children with love and understanding. Often the children respond by resisting such attempts at emotional closeness. The myth of instant love and its unrealistic and difficult expectations contributes to a second myth - that of the 'cruel stepmother'. The stepmother may feel under pressure from her partner, who may feel guilty if the children are unhappy, and therefore pushes for 'instant love'. In addition, she may feel that she is being judged by the children, her partner and other family members, neighbours and society as a whole. This puts tremendous pressure on her to immediately love her stepchildren. Naturally, this is impossible as she may just be getting to know her stepchildren - and at this stage she may not even like them!

The cruel stepmother

A stepmother is confronted by social and cultural contradictions. On the one hand we are told stepmothers are cruel. On the other hand we are told that all women love children, and thus stepmothers should instantly love their stepchildren. No other relationship has this expectation of instant love and affection. The diagram over shows how this can become a vicious circle.

A further expectation on a stepmother is that she should not

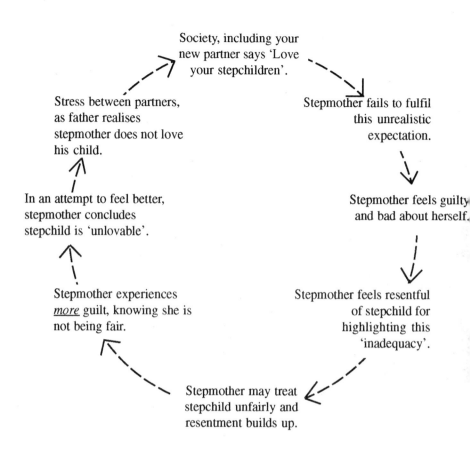

only love her stepchildren, but love them as much as her birth children. Clearly this is highly unlikely at the start of a relationship, but it is possible over time to come to like and love stepchildren, and to be a supportive friend.

It can be a real advantage for stepchildren to have a more objective adult (such as a step-parent), if their parents can accept an objective viewpoint, which at times may be critical of both stepchild and the parents way of dealing with things.

You may want to discuss the differences in feelings with stepchildren if you think they can handle the information.

For example, you may suggest that we feel differently because our relationship is different and it will take time for it to grow and develop.

You may want to let the children take the lead in this step (similar to talking about sex). If a child questions "how come stepdaddy or stepmummy likes his/her children better", then it is better to respond positively and openly to the stepchildren rather than deny differences. This can be very relieving to the children since they probably also love their parents more than their step-parents but may feel guilty for doing so.

A consequence of trying to pretend that there are feelings of affection toward a stepchild when they do not exist is that the step-parents often feel very self conscious and inhibited in expressing affection and other positive feelings to his or her own children.

Children are also put in a bind as a result of this instant love expectation. They may feel guilty if they do not love a step-parent or if they do, they may feel disloyal to their absent parent.

The cruel stepmother myth has endured for centuries in all cultures in fairy stories such as Cinderella and Snow White. The theme is the same in each culture. The stepmother prefers her own children and attempts to alienate her husband from his children.

However, stepfathers prefer their own children too, so why not a myth about them? True there are wicked stepfathers in Shakespeare's plays and Dickens' novels but none embedded in children's fairy tales in the same way as the stepmother. It seems to boil down to the fact that western society and children expect more parenting from mothers than from fathers. If a mother figure lets a child down, there is more hurt and more anger. This is written into the literature and is handed down from generation to generation. And the power of the myth is strong.

Children seem able to discard the myth much sooner than their stepmothers.

How to become more comfortable with the myth

1. Accept the fact that parents have different feelings for their own children and for stepchildren. If feelings are allowed to develop over time through trust and respect for each other they will come more easily.

2. Accept the fact that step-parents will be unfair to stepchildren occasionally, sometimes because they are cross or upset, sometimes because they are unaware they are behaving differently.

3. Parenting is not easy, even with our birth children. It is natural to resent the work or cost of stepchildren on occasion.

4. Do not expect extra appreciation from stepchildren for work. They take for granted, just as all children do, that parents will do things for them - it's a form of acceptance.

5. Beware of displacement of anger. Stepchildren are a natural target if you are angry at your partner. Direct your anger at your partner if that is where the anger lies.

6. Do not hold back anger at a stepchild if that is where the

anger really is. Holding back anger is poisonous to all relationships. Children can handle anger if expressed directly and non-blaming (see owning our feelings p67).

7. Remember that it is easier to argue about the stepchildren and blame them for things going wrong in the couple relationship than it is to acknowledge that things are not going well in that relationship.

Competition for love and affection

Time is a very precious commodity and this is particularly so when considering the competing needs of all members of a stepfamily, whether resident or non-resident. It is helpful to think about competition quite specifically and how it is expressed and managed. You may have found some complex ways of handling these matters, or you may be wondering what to do about them.

There may be many competing groups in a stepfamily:

1. Stepmother vs stepchildren, for dad's affection when non-resident children visit.

2. Stepfather vs mother's children, for mother's affection.

3. Each partner's children competing with each other, for affection from parent, step-parent, or grandparents.

4. The stepcouple vs all the children, wanting adult attention.

By accepting and understanding that such rivalries are common, the situation will not seem so overwhelming and attention can be given to figuring out ways to reduce the factions.

In families, couples do things alone as well as together. Children often have special time with one of their parents alone. Stepfamilies are no different, it's just that there are more combinations of adults and children who want to spend time together.

Competition between stepsiblings occurs just as competition can arise between siblings in any family. It is inevitable that some competition will develop as children in the family attempt to ensure that they will have a place in the family system. For many children their place in the family changes within the stepfamily - from youngest to oldest, or eldest to middle. From only child to one of five, from only girl or boy to one of several.

It can be hard at first for children to share their parent with a stepbrother or sister. You can ease this by giving your own children some special attention, reassuring them that they are still as important and giving them an opportunity to express any resentment about their stepsiblings.

As in any family, competition is most likely to occur over practical issues where differences can be greater in a stepfamily if the stepchild gets lots of extra and lavish gifts from an absent parent.

Equal treatment in terms of expenditures within the stepfamily may be possible, keeping spending roughly equal, but not necessarily the same. If one child gets a bike, it doesn't mean the other one has to have one also. But it can e hard when some children in the stepfamily consistently get re from outside the stepfamily household. As children get er they realise that love, affection and gifts are different it can be painful if the gifts are not openly shared.

Stepmothers

Experience and research show that stepmothers tend to have a more difficult time in their role than stepfathers because they often spend more time with the children and because western society still expects women to be more nurturing and more affective with children. The expectation that 'all women are born mothers' sets up stepmothers for possible failure.

Stepmothers are often ill-prepared for the initial rejection they experience. They may jump in too fast, especially stepmothers with no parenting experience of their own. Since most stepmothers want to be good parents, they may find it difficult to express negative feeling towards their stepchildren. Often they are puzzled by questions of whether or not they should impose their own rules, disregard the child's present habits, or accept what has already been established before they entered the family.

Another difficult part of the stepmother's role can occur when she receives enquiries about the child and does not have the appropriate information e.g. questions about medical history, school records etc. Such situations can undermine her confidence and she may feel awkward and helpless. Society expects mothers to know all the answers about their children. However, if a stepmother realises that her role and function is different from that of a birth mother, she no longer has to compete with her or with her role.

Stepfathers

Stepfathers also experience some unique problems. They may be cast in the role of an intruder, since a stepfather often moves into the home of a mother and her children. Accordingly, the stepfather needs to move carefully to establish a sense of his place and belonging. Men may not have as many fantasies about stepfatherhood as stepmothers do, because typically caring for children and focusing on children's needs has been considered 'women's work'. The first difficulty stepfathers often encounter may arise from the child's fear that he will 'steal' the mother's attention and deprive the child of love and affection, as well as trying to replace the child's father.

Some major areas of conflict or of special concern to the stepfather may include:
+ Division of labour - who is going to do what?
+ Personal space - finding his own place in this new stepfamily household (especially if he has moved in to the mother's house).
+ Discipline.

In looking at who does what, the stepfather may have to take on parenting tasks and responsibilities that he did not have before, and there may be others in the home who take on responsibilities that used to be his. Personal space is reduced now that there is someone else in the home, and often the stepfather feels that he is on someone else's turf and is uncomfortable establishing personal space for himself. He may also have to contend with the ghost of a birth father.

Since he is now a part of the new family unit, he may be expected to discipline the children in a variety of ways. Often he is unsure about how much to discipline, when to discipline, and whether or not his partner supports his efforts at discipline. These are things that the couple needs to talk about. It is important to decide how much the stepfather is to be involved with discipline, if at all. It is usually helpful for step-parents to develop a relationship and mutual respect with the stepchildren before they begin to act as disciplinarians.

Many stepfathers feel that they have a lot of responsibility but little or no power and appreciation. Stepfathers may react to this lack of control by becoming either authoritarian or withdrawn. Stepfathers may also feel guilty because they are spending more time with their stepchildren than they are with their own children. They may resent a loss of contact with their own children, and thus distance themselves from their stepchildren because of their sadness and guilt.

Research has found that stepfathers spend more time thinking about their roles and responsibilities than do birth fathers. Stepfathers are often self-conscious and self-critical, and rate themselves lower as parents than their partners or stepchildren rate them.

Stepfathers may also experience similar feelings to those of stepmothers. They often feel lost, confused, unappreciated and uncertain of how to play their role as step-parent .

Tips for step-parents

1. Being a stepmother or stepfather is different from being a mother or father. Don't expect them to be the same. There are also differences between being a resident and non-resident step-parent.

2. Create a partnership with your partner. Clarify your roles so that each of you has clear expectations of the other.

3. Learn to live with the reality of ex-partners. Do not criticise the absent parent, especially in front of the stepchild, as they may experience any such criticism as a criticism of themselves. Support your stepchild talking about their other parent. Such discussions help maintain continuity in the child's life and reduce loyalty conflicts for them.

4. Be patient as relationships take time to develop. Love does not occur instantly. Be patient and allow the child time to accept you. Share yourself with your stepchildren but let the children decide the pace. Spending time together and talking with one another will help the gradual development of the emotional ties between you and your stepchildren.

5. Develop a relationship with your stepchildren before attempting discipline.

6. Remember that to love a stepchild as one's own may not be possible, to like and to respect the stepchild is a more reasonable expectation.

7. Don't blame yourself for everything that goes wrong. Step-parents should remember that some problems will be related to a child's growth and development, rather than being unique to family circumstances.

8. Your life satisfactions need to be derived from many sources. Your stepchildren need not be your exclusive focus, even if you are a resident step-parent. Outside activities beyond the family, such as work, friends and hobbies are enhancing to family life, as well as time for you and your partner.

9. Be discreet with open expressions of physical affection in the presence of the children. When you hug or kiss your partner in front of the children, it may be helpful to show some affection towards the child in some way, such as a pat on the shoulder; whatever would be appropriate to the child's age and to the relationship.

10. Stepfathers may find themselves attracted to their stepdaughters. Remember that even birth fathers may experience sexual feelings towards their daughters. The important thing is to recognise that we have many feelings we do not and should not act upon. It is helpful to set clear limits in the stepfamily on dress, nudity and privacy.

Tips for parents

Parents may often feel a great deal of guilt and other strong emotions after the divorce or death of a partner. They may feel caught in the middle between the children and the new partner. They may be feeling: "after my partner died, the children were all I had left", "my partner didn't care, but I did", or "I'll make it up to the children for separating from their mum or their dad". They may become overly protective towards their children.

A sense of failure in their first relationship may make them more determined than ever to create the perfect family next time. These feelings can create pressures for the stepfamily.

After creating a stepfamily, the parent may place unrealistic expectations on their new partner as well as on the children to behave as a 'real family'. Perhaps the birth parent is tired of the sole responsibility for parenting and is anxious to share it with the new partner. In some instances the parents may have assured the children that they will always come first; this gives them a confusing message when a new partner comes along.

Since children may have had a major share of the parent's attention in the lone parent household, they may have become possessive of the parent and may deliberately engage in behaviour that demands attention and is designed to drive away the step-parent. They may become angry, sullen, withdrawn or manipulative. Often they test the parent's affection and love for them. How can parents deal effectively with these feelings? Some guidelines follow:

1. Remember that as the parent, yours is a key position of authority and responsibility. You will feel this most strongly in the beginning of your new stepfamily as your children and your partner (their step-parent) adjust to each other. You are in a pivotal position because you are the only adult who is part of both elements in the stepfamily: the parent/child bond and the couple relationship.
2. Share information about your attitude of child-rearing and discipline openly, honestly and clearly with your partner as soon as possible.

3. Work together as a couple and support one another as actively as possible. Your new partner will probably handle many situations differently from you, particularly if he or she has never had children. Show support for him or her in front of the children. Sort out your differences and reach agreement in private.

4. Help your partner gradually assume his or her authority with your children. You can't and won't be there all the time to act as arbitrator, grant final permission, or deny the requests of your children. The way your children respond to their step-parent depends greatly on the credibility, trust and authority that you give to him or her in front of the children.

5. Accept the differences between your household and the other households where your children and stepchildren are members. As you establish your new house rules, you need to realise that things will be different in the other home(s); that does not necessarily make one household right or wrong. The children will learn to adjust to and accommodate the difference.

6. Examine your motives and try to avoid acting from a sense of guilt. Accept the past as past. Live in the present and do what is best for each member of the stepfamily.

7. Treat children and stepchildren equally in terms of rules, rewards and responsibilities. There should be one set of rules for all the children in your household, even though some may only be there for short periods of time. This gives the children a sense of belonging and reduces any concerns that they may be viewed as outsiders or guests. Make certain that fun things happen regularly, not just when the non-resident children are present.

8. Remind your children often that your love for them has not changed. The relationship you have with your new partner is _different_ from the one you have with them; it is not better or stronger. Let them know that your own unique, individual and special relationship with each of them will continue.

9. Spend time with your children individually and collectively. Keep building and nurturing your relationship with them.

10. Encourage your partner to spend time with your children individually and collectively. Encourage the growth of these relationships.

11. Spend time alone with your new partner. Maintain your relationship with him or her by planning special times together on a regular basis.

Positive aspects of living in step

1. The children now have two adults in the household who can serve as role models.
2. The step-parent may have a more objective view of the stepchildren and may be able to initiate change or provide insights into the children's behaviour. He or she may come into the household as an 'objective observer' and be helpful in the parenting process.
3. Step-parents can provide friendship, nurturing and emotional support for the children.
4. The new couple provides a positive adult model for children to see that two adults can care for each other and live compatibly together.
5. Children can learn from step-parents and from stepsiblings. More caring people in a child's life can provide more interaction and support.
6. Children can observe and learn from different family lifestyles and value systems. There are varied opportunities for them to explore new experiences and develop new skills and hobbies.
7. Children's flexibility and adaptability can be increased by living in a stepfamily. They can learn to be more tolerant of differences, and better able to negotiate and compromise, and deal with conflict.
8. A special bond of closeness can be created by working together and solving difficult and challenging problems.
9. Adults and children in stepfamilies have an opportunity to confront and solve many challenging and complex problems, thereby enhancing their sense of self-esteem and competence.

Owning our feelings

We often blame others for our feelings without being aware that we are doing it. Imagine your different feelings if somebody made the following pairs of statements to you:

"You're so selfish."
"I feel upset because you didn't help me with the washing-up."

"Your behaviour drives me to distraction."
"I don't like it when you talk to me like that."

"You never think of me."
"I get really worried when you stay out later than we agreed."

In each "you" statement the speaker is blaming the other person and labelling them when in fact the speaker is upset about something. There are a number of problems with blaming and labelling others for your upset:

♦ Blaming messages escalate the tension all around. The person who is blamed is unlikely to change their behaviour. The speaker will continue to feel angry and frustrated and the person blamed is likely to feel that way as well.

♦ 'You' messages do not communicate clearly what it is we are upset about and what we want the other person to change in their behaviour. "You never think of me" could mean anything and the listener may genuinely have no idea what is wanted of them.

♦ Labelling 'you' messages can become self-fulfilling

prophecies. The more we call somebody selfish, the more they are likely to believe they are selfish and act selfishly. Younger children in particular are overawed by the power of our language. If we say to a child that they are clumsy/stupid/selfish or whatever, they are likely to believe us - especially if we use the label repeatedly - because we are their all-powerful and all-knowing parents. But the repetition of such labels can affect anyone (young people and adults) in a similar way.

'I' messages have many advantages:

• They communicate clearly how we feel and what we want. "I get really worried when you stay out later than we agreed" is a clear statement that can lead to a simple conversation to resolve the problem.

• 'I' messages avoid the danger of labelling. In an 'I' message we separate out the other person from their actions. So we say what it is we like or don't like about their behaviour, rather than making a statement about them as people.

• 'I' messages model owning and expressing our feelings. The more we are able to own our feelings in this way the more our children will learn by example to own and express their feelings.

Anger

Anger is an interesting feeling. When we feel anger we mostly feel it is caused by someone else - "You made me feel angry". Contrast this with sadness, for example. We can more easily own our sadness - "I feel sad" without needing to find somebody else as the cause of our sadness. It takes time to learn to own our anger, and allow others to own theirs without feeling personally blamed for it. Examples of angry 'I' messages might be:

"I felt so angry when you broke my favourite bowl."
"I feel angry when you refuse to talk to your stepmother/ father."

If we explore feelings of anger we often find that other feelings lie hidden behind the anger. In the examples above it is quite likely that sadness lies behind the anger, sadness about the breakage and sadness when your child doesn't speak to your partner, a loved one. Very often when we feel anger it is in fact a cover for another feeling. It can help to identify and express that feeling behind the anger rather than just staying with the anger.

Another way of expressing anger is just to let off steam at nobody in particular. Thus you can shout to the sky: "I feel so angry I could scream", some people pound pillows, kick the door, or do some physical exercise to get the angry feelings out of their system. Evasive action is generally more useful than dumping your anger on another person.

Summary

In stepfamilies, as in nuclear families, the couple relationship is of prime importance. One way of enhancing this relationship is by sharing expectations before creating the stepfamily, and at intervals after its formation.

After a divorce or loss of a parent through death, children usually feel angry and confused. They need reassurance and specific information about what changes will take place in their lives.

In forming a stepfamily the couple need to talk about the changes that will take place for them, how they will relate to former partners, and how they wish the new family to function.

There are stages in the development of a stepfamily with accompanying tasks of letting go of past relationships and developing new ones, through learning about each other.

There are both unique challenges and difficulties facing step-parents and parents as well as positive things that are part of stepfamily life. No adult role in the stepfamily is simple. Each of you faces daily responsibilities that require the utmost patience, tolerance and maturity. Being able to ask clearly for what you want from one another is very important. The emotional support that you give each other is invaluable.

There are many positive aspects of living in a stepfamily for children, new opportunities for developing skills, self-esteem and competence, and closeness with an additional adult who cares about them.

Notes to myself on what I have learned

4

Children and stepfamilies

*"It's just so unfair. Ryan and Zoe get to see their Dad
and I have to share my toys and bedroom when they
visit. But Ben and I haven't seen our Dad for years.
Sometimes he doesn't even send a birthday card."*

*"I'm sort of looking forward to the new baby. But
what if Mum is too busy with the baby and Ian likes it
more than me?"*

*"It's a bit hard to know what I think about
stepfamilies. When I'm with my Mum I'm the youngest
and I have to do what everyone else says 'cos Jim's
boys are older than me. And when I'm at my Dad's
then I'm the oldest and he says I have to look after the
little ones. It's strange sometimes."*

Children's reactions to forming a stepfamily

This section focuses on children in stepfamilies. Trying to
understand and appreciate their special concerns and feelings
is essential for creating a good atmosphere for your
stepfamily and exercising effective discipline.

All children, whether nuclear, step, adopted, or foster, are
concerned from time to time, with anxiety and fears of:
* Abandonment
* Loss of love
* Bodily harm

A stepfamily can heighten fears of being abandoned or losing love. Earlier on we suggested things that parents could do to alleviate these fears at the time of the death, divorce or separation. We are going to make some similar suggestions of things to do around the time of the formation of the stepfamily and afterwards. Some of you may have already found ways of helping children accept the new situation.

Let's make some general points. Some stepchildren feel positive anticipation toward a new step-parent, but they may also, and at the same time, view them with a great deal of suspicion. They may feel angry at the step-parent's intrusion, and jealous of the attention the step-parent receives from their parent. Underneath, the children usually hope that things will work out well.

The children have experienced a double loss; first, the end of their family and the loss of one parent from the household and; second, the end of a single-parent household and the loss of some of the attention from one of their parents. Once again, they must adjust to a situation which is not of their choosing. The following may be a typical sequence of events and the resulting stress the children experience when going from a nuclear family to a stepfamily.

The parents decide to separate and the father moves out. The children still love him and want to see him. They may fear that he no longer loves them and that is why he left. They still want and love their mother, with whom they now live. They may become very close to her and very dependant upon her for closeness. A new partner for her may alter all this, just as they are becoming adjusted to the fact of living with one parent and visiting the other. Their loyalties are confused.

When the mother forms a new relationship, the mother may see the new partner as bringing a new security or a new threat or both. If they are able to continue to see their father, they may feel secure enough to risk forming a relationship with the new step-parent. On the other hand, they may feel he threatens whatever security they had begun to experience in the new household and they may fear their mother has stopped loving or wanting them. Their behaviour may become very difficult as they test how much their mother really loves them and will keep on being their mother.

When their father forms a new partnership, the children experience another set of similar feelings. That may seem like another desertion and they may fear that a stepmother will come between them and their father. They may fear he will not continue to want or love them, and he is also likely to experience various tests of his affection and caring for the children.

The loss of a parent either by death or divorce may be regarded by children as a betrayal. They cling to the other parent to be protected and cared for. The arrival of a step-parent on the scene may seem to be a further betrayal.

Stepmothers seem to be particularly suspect by children, who see them as coming between them and their father or between them and the memory or place of their mother. This is because of the expectations that mothers will do most of the caring. Whether a stepmother is gentle and kind or harsh and hostile, the children may feel they have been wronged.

Children often experience fear that after separation or divorce, one of their parents will hurt or reject them if they have a good relationship with the other parent. They often fear reporting a good visit when they get home in case the parent at home resents this. Yet, studies show that children who are encouraged to have an ongoing relationship with both their parents are more able to relax and develop a relationship with a step-parent - if they are not threatened with the loss of either parent they do not perceive the step-parent as taking the parent's place.

'Visiting' children

A major source of stepfamily tension is getting to know stepchildren who are not with you the majority of the time. Since these children are usually the father's children, we will discuss an example from that perspective. It is often a problem for the father to decide how much time he should spend with his own children when they are with him.

For many families it works out well if the father spends some time alone with his children. They may go somewhere together or he may simply find a way to read or play with them at special times in between times the stepfamily spends together as a group.

This allows the children to feel that their relationship with their father is still important and they tend to feel less competitive or jealous of their stepmother or of stepbrothers and sisters. It also makes it easier for a father to accept his stepchildren if he can have some time alone with his own children. This reduces his guilt and helps him feel that he is able to be both father and stepfather without making anyone feel cheated or left out.

Time alone is equally important for each sub-system in a stepfamily: for the couple, for the mother and her children, father and his children, stepmother and stepchildren, stepfather and stepchildren, and mother and father with any new children born into the stepfamily.

Even after the children have had answers to the major questions which they ask when one or both of their parents forms a new partnership, such as - will they lose contact with one of their parents, how will they fit into the new family - certain stresses can still occur.

Stresses for children in stepfamilies

1. Hearing their birth parents argue over the phone or at the door, or say negative things about each other. They may wonder if they are to blame for this.

2. Not being able or allowed to see their other parent, and resenting their step-parent for this.

3. Feeling blamed for everything that goes wrong.

4. Hearing their parent and step-parent fight, and fearing that this stepcouple relationship will break up.

5. Believing their parents do more for stepsiblings than for them.

6. Having stepsiblings messing up their belongings and intruding into their space and privacy.

7. Dealing with feelings of not being wanted, often testing to see if either stepfamily household really wants them.

8. Feeling angry and depressed and wishing it could all be the way it was before the death or divorce.

9. Having a step-parent telling them what to do and resenting this.

10. Feeling that it's up to them to make the new stepfamily household work.

11. Feeling like pawns and messengers tossed between their birth parents who are still feeling bitter and angry towards each other.

12. Adjusting to all the new rules in one or both stepfamily households.

Not all stepchildren will experience all of these stresses, but many will have some of these feelings and experiences. And not all stepchildren in the same stepfamily will feel the same way about things. Talking with them about how they are feeling, even if they seem not to respond, can do much to alleviate their worry. Keeping them informed of family plans or changes in plans for visits can help them feel more involved and more secure.

It is helpful to remember that children may be very difficult, disruptive or irritating at times of major family changes; some of this is to be expected. Assuring them of their place in your life, spending time with them, and listening to their feelings will help to make the transition smoother.

Building children's self-esteem

Because of the changes children in stepfamilies have been through, they often feel they are different from other children, and that something is wrong with them and their family. From studies about children in stepfamilies we know that their self-esteem is often lowered by the changes, some of which may have been traumatic for them. The studies also indicate that children usually grow up normally and well in stepfamilies, but they may need some extra help from parents at crucial times, as may any child.

If children are given encouragement, credit and recognition for the things they do well and for the contribution they make to the stepfamily, they will have much less need to act out and gain recognition and attention for misbehaviour. Often stepfamily life is confusing and hectic. It is easy to overlook the positive contributions children make to stepfamily life. However, the encouragement or praise that you give your stepchildren and children on a daily basis will contribute to a strong sense of self-worth, as well as encourage them to grow up to be emotionally secure individuals. Below are some tips on helping children. Followed by a letter which you might want to blow up as a poster to put on the fridge door!

Guidelines to giving praise

1. Say how you feel about your child's or stepchild's pleasing behaviour. For example, expressing thanks, relief, excitement or happiness.

2. Follow this with a specific description of something which pleased you. For example, "I am so pleased that you remembered to do that without being asked".

3. The message should also describe the benefits that result from a pleasing behaviour. It is helpful for children to know exactly how their behaviour has helped someone else in the family. Also, it is important to look for and encourage on a regular basis the positive things that children are doing. It is much easier to be critical, to comment on negative things, and to try to change a child's

behaviour. However, it brings us closer to our stepchildren and children and enhances their self-esteem if we can give them encouragement that is specific, consistent and shared on a regular basis.

Practical tips for building children's self-esteem

1. Look for behaviour in your children and stepchildren that you like, even if they are small things and not particularly unusual.

2. Remember that you cannot encourage or praise children too much. Attempt to share some positive words and affectionate gestures with your child or stepchild on a daily basis.

3. Sometimes a pat on the back, a quick hug or an arm around the shoulders can be the best way to help a child's self-esteem, and to express your appreciation for something that was helpful to you or the stepfamily.

4. Remember that simple activities such as playing cards, reading or watching TV help to build a good relationship with a child without demanding too much of either of you.

5. Find a little time during each week, or at each visit, when you can spend a few moments alone with each child. It may only be a few minutes when you help them tie their shoes or manage the toothpaste. During this time, listen to your children or stepchildren and ask them about things that have been happening with them or with their friends, at school or around the home.

6. To help children develop a sense of belonging and commitment to the stepfamily, ask them for opinions,

A letter from your child/stepchild:

This is about **me**.................................

❂ Set limits for me. I know very well that I ought not to have all I ask for. I am only testing you and trying to find out what the limits are.

❂ Be firm with me. I prefer it. It let's me know where I stand.

❂ Lead me rather than force me. If you always force me, it teaches me that power is all that counts. I will argue sometimes, but I will respond more readily to being led.

❂ Be consistent. Inconsistency confuses me and makes me try harder to get away with everything I can.

❂ Make promises that you will be able to keep. That will encourage my trust in you.

❂ Remember that I am trying to provoke you when I say and do things just to upset you. If you fall for my provocations, I'll try for more such victories.

❂ Keep calm when I say "I hate you." I don't mean it. It's what I say when I'm feeling angry or when I just want you to feel sorry for what you have done.

❂ Help me feel big rather than small. When I feel small I try to make up for it by behaving 'big'.

❂ Let me do the things I can do for myself. When you do them for me, it makes me feel like a baby, and I may continue to be unnecessarily dependent on you.

❂ Correct me in private. I'll take much more notice if you talk quietly with me in private rather than with other people present.

❂ Take whatever action you need when I misbehave, but discuss my behaviour when the conflict has subsided. In the heat of conflict for some reason my hearing is not very good and my co-operation is even worse.

❂ Talk with me rather than preach to me. Help me feel that my mistakes are not sins. I have to learn to make mistakes without feeling that I am no good.

❂ Talk firmly without nagging. If you nag I shall protect myself by appearing deaf. Let my wrong behaviour go without asking me to explain it. I often really don't know why I did it.

❂ Accept as much as you can of what I am able to tell you. I am easily frightened into telling lies if my honesty is taxed too much.

ideas, and feelings about stepfamily problems. The other part of this is to encourage children to be responsible members of the stepfamily by offering them opportunities to take on responsibilities for themselves and around the home. This could be very small things, according to age and ability, and also willingness. If you make suggestions, the opening is there to begin to make changes.

Summary

This section has covered some of the satisfactions and difficulties in being a step-parent and parent in a stepfamily. We have also covered some of the stresses that children in stepfamilies experience.

Change in families can be difficult for everyone. Being sensitive to the stresses, combined with an ability and willingness to listen to the children, will greatly enhance their adjustment.

There are specific guidelines for giving positive reinforcement to children, and following them will help create a more satisfactory and happy climate for everyone in the family.

Notes to myself on what I have learned

5

Building relationships with our children and stepchildren

"I like it when John takes me to football and stays to watch me play. Mum's not very keen on football."

"I wish she'd just understand that when I go to see my Dad I want to see him on my own some of the time."

"They treat my home like a hotel but they don't behave like guests, more like invading forces."

Feelings and behaviour

There is a difference between 'feelings' and 'behaviour'. While feelings are not 'right' or 'wrong', behaviour can be constructive or destructive in nature. As well as being sensitive to the feelings of your children and stepchildren, it is sometimes necessary to set limits on their behaviour.

The need for discipline or limit setting is necessary in all families. However, in stepfamilies discipline is more complicated.

Unless the step-parent has been living with the stepchild since his or her birth, the two adults have completely different relationships with the children in the family. They may also have different ideas, values and standards for children's behaviour in general. One parent, the birth parent, will already be involved in disciplining his or her own children. The step-parent is a newcomer to that, and many parents and step-parents have very mixed feelings about the step-parent's role as disciplinarian. Many step-parents are tested over and over before they are accepted as having authority, and during that period the step-parent may not feel the parent is giving the kind of support that is needed.

Effective discipline needs a foundation of respect and a bond of affection. Earning respect and building affection takes time. Therefore, discipline cannot be rushed. In this section we will be talking about some of the ways in which a step-parent can create a foundation of respect and a bond of affection in the early stages of stepfamily life.

A study of the ways in which stepfathers discipline their stepchildren found that when the stepfather spent time initially developing a relationship, doing things for and with the child, the discipline that followed this 'befriending process' was more readily acceptable. The gradual process of 'making friends' with stepchildren and then moving slowly towards disciplining does seem to make it easier for the step-parent to be accepted into the stepfamily and for the stepfamily to develop its own way of doing things.

As was mentioned earlier, discipline is most effective when there is a bond of affection between adult and child. Approval is a powerful reinforcer in stepfamily relationships. If stepchildren want the respect, affection or support of their step-parent they will be more inclined to respond to their discipline. As a step-parent becomes more important to the child, the desire to please and work with the step-parent will increase.

The parent can serve as a kind of go-between in the early stages for the step-parent and child, by helping each to understand the behaviour of the other. However, the parent must not take this role too long since doing so may put them in the role of a referee. It may also reduce the opportunities for step-parents and stepchildren to communicate and negotiate between themselves. In the initial phase of a stepfamily, the responsibility for providing discipline rests with the birth parent since that adult already has the authority with his/her children.

Tips on building relationships with children in your stepfamily

- Listen.
- Allow time for the child to accept you.
- Notice what you like about the children and what they do.
- Spend time with them.
- Be truthful.
- Be reliable in an emergency.
- Allow some talk about their absent parent.
- Share a favourite book or game.
- Teach a skill.
- Give a special responsibility.
- Give an honest compliment.
- Ask about their day and interests.
- Explain the money situation.
- Talk to your partner.

Values

Values are the beliefs that guide our actions. Often we may not be aware of our values because we have developed them and lived with them over such a long period that they seem self-evident, as if they are part of the way the world is rather than personal beliefs that we hold. Examples of values are:

- I will not let my children play with guns and war toys (because I am a pacifist).

- Young children need at least ten hours sleep each night.
- Anger is a destructive emotion so people must learn to hold it in.
- The house must be kept tidy.
- Young people should not have sexual relationships below ..... years of age.
- I don't believe in smacking children or any physical punishment.

Many of the bitterest conflicts in families (as in the world at large) arise over values. Such conflicts often come to the fore as children get older. When children are younger they tend to accept parental values without question. As they go out into the world they come into contact with other people's values (such as teachers at school and their peers). They have to start deciding for themselves what their own values are. It can be difficult for parents to allow their children to decide on these, especially when the values that their children take on clash with parents' deeply held values.

However, forcing our values on our children tends to lead them to either rebel against ours in protest or to appear to accept them while resenting the fact that they haven't been given a choice. It is more useful to model our values to our children by the way we lead our lives and leave them free to decide what they believe in for themselves. This way, paradoxically, they are more likely to freely choose to take on our values or to ask us for our opinions and feel free to follow them, knowing that opinions will be given with no strings attached.

Managing time in stepfamilies

Time is a limited commodity. And stepfamily members have many competing demands on their time. You need to manage your time well in order to give time to all the different stepfamily relationships. You need:

- Time on your own.
- Time with your partner.
- Time with each of your children (individually).
- Time with each of your stepchildren (individually).
- Time together as a stepfamily.
- Time for extended family - such as grandparents and step-grandparents.

There will be periods when you will need to devote more time to one relationship than another. For example, when you have formed a new couple relationship you will need to spend time with your partner working out the details of life together. At such times of transition, children (especially younger ones) are likely to want more time with their parent for reassurance that they are still loved and that there is still a central place for them in the stepfamily. You will want to make yourself available to any stepchildren so that you can begin the task of developing a relationship which is a first step toward taking on the step-parenting role.

Time on your own

You can easily be overwhelmed by the number of relationships that there are in your stepfamily and forget to take time to be on your own. It is important to find the time to do the things that you enjoy doing on your own - whether it's taking a hot bath, curling up in bed with a book or giving yourself a special treat. If you feel contented in yourself, then you will be all the more able to enjoy the members of your stepfamily.

Time with your partner

We will discuss the importance of the couple relationship in Chapter 8 (Strengthening the stepcouple). You and your partner need to find time alone to do things together. The stronger your relationship, the stronger the stepfamily as a whole. It is easy for the demands of running a stepfamily to encroach on your time to such an extent that you find that time for your relationship is squeezed out. You will probably have to plan to spend time alone together to make sure it actually happens! You may decide to:

♦ **Spend some time away together from the household each week** doing something you both enjoy. You may not have had time to develop common interests and so you may need to take turns choosing the activities. This will allow each of you to experience what the other enjoys and will help you find out what interests you have in common. You may need to make a rule not to discuss stepfamily issues as it is so easy for them to encroach on times that are meant for rest and relaxation. If you have younger children you will, of course, need to pay for a babysitter or organise a babysitting swap. It is worth the effort of organising this time for you and your partner!

♦ **Arrange to have 20 minutes of relaxed time alone together every other day** (apart from sleeping in the same bed which doesn't count). This could include talking, cooking, gardening, listening to music, watching TV, snuggling together in bed. You may need to work to prevent the children from encroaching on this time. A sign on the bedroom door "Do not knock unless you're bleeding" may be part of your strategy to help them learn to respect your privacy (in the way you would respect their privacy).

♦ **Talk together for at least 30 minutes a week about the running of your household.** This is important because you are both bringing different values and expectations into the new family home, rather than being able to build them up together over time. Decide on the most important matters to discuss, postponing to later times other matters that need changing. Choose specific issues that can be easily identified and can be changed realistically, for example:
> Finishing homework before playing or watching TV
> Table manners
> Taking off muddy shoes before coming into the house
> Taking turns drying the dishes
> No eating and drinking in the living room.

You may like to discuss:
♦ The possibility of different rules when there are more or fewer people in the home (e.g. when stepchildren are visiting or away at their other parent's home).
♦ Supporting the step-parent when they are left in sole charge of stepchildren (in the way that you would back up any childcare person coming in to the home).

Over time these parental responsibilities will be more equally shared and both parents will comfortably share these roles.

Time with your children

If you have more than one child you may sometimes do things with them together. However, it is also important to spend one-to-one time with each of them even if that only happens once a week. Organise to spend at least 15 or 20 minutes a week doing something *fun* with each of them. If you live apart from your children and only see them on rare occasions, stay in touch with them by letter and/or telephone and ensure that you have light-hearted as well as serious interactions with them. Make arrangements with your children ahead of time so they can look forward to the arrangement. Remember to involve your partner in your plans to spend time on your own with each of your children in order to minimise any disruption it may cause to the rest of the family. Ensure that such plans are adhered to, and do not threaten to abandon such times as a punishment for misbehaviour.

Your children may not know what they want to do or may want something that is impossible. Make the best possible arrangements in the circumstances. Ensure that your child knows how long this 'special time' will last - for example, "We can ride our bikes until 5.00pm." or "There'll be time for one game". And if your child is upset when the 'special time' is over, take it as an appreciation of how much they enjoyed the time and so do not want it to end. Acknowledge their upset (as we discussed in the section 'Acknowledging feelings' on p37-42) rather than trying to talk them out of their feelings of upset or getting angry. Your anger is likely to sour the memory of the time spent together. Over time a child will learn to contain the disappointment felt when a good time comes to an end, especially if they know that special time will be happening again soon.

Time with your stepchildren

This is just as important for developing a relationship with your stepchildren as it is for maintaining (and developing) the relationship with your birth children. The principles of spending time together are essentially the same. The main difference to underline is that you will need to start by building a relationship with your stepchildren. It may help if at first you do not plan time ahead with your stepchild but wait until the relationship develops to the point where your stepchild wants to spend such time with you or you think it would be appropriate to do so.

The parent needs to stay out of the way to enable you to build your own relationship with your stepchildren. It may be difficult for the parent to 'let go'. They may feel the need to intervene to 'help the two of you get along' whereas in fact you need time to be on your own. If it is hard for the parent to step back, then it might be a good idea for them to be away from the house while you have your special time with their children - your stepchildren.

There may be resistance on the part of your stepchildren to build such a relationship with you, their step-parent. They may have such strong, negative feelings about you and what you represent that they are not willing to accept you. Although it may not be easy, it is useful if you can continue to show your stepchildren that you are available to them and want to build a relationship with them. Try not to take the negative feelings they direct at you too personally. Try to recognise that they need to get their anger, resentment or frustration out and use you as a 'target', and that they will be able to become friends with you when those feelings are through. However, such feelings may last for years and may not be resolved until they have become young adults and left the stepfamily home .

Special time - following your child's lead

We have introduced the concept of special time in the section above. Special time is a name some people give to the period of time that they spend doing what their children want. For special time to go well there are a few simple principles to follow:

♦ The child chooses what to do during special time. If they choose a game that you do not enjoy playing, summon up as much energy as you can to throw yourself enthusiastically into the game.

♦ When playing the game, hold back on making suggestions as to how the game ought to be played or what you ought to do next. As adults we tend to organise our children's lives much of the time and they really appreciate the opportunity of complete freedom that special time gives them. It is not as easy as it sounds to give up our adult control and just follow our children's lead. Do try it and see how each child responds.

♦ Ensure that there is lots of pleasure and laughter. Sometimes, when playing with a young person, the game which started out as fun can become stale or overly serious. Making a fool of yourself is one effective way of bringing laughter back into a game. If you are playing football you could pretend to kick the ball and miss it and playfully act upset as a result, or if you are playing a board game you could surreptitiously cheat (in such a way that the young person clearly sees you) and then light-heartedly deny it, or be upset about being found out. The ensuing laughter can brighten up the atmosphere when you and the young person are playing a game that has lost its spark and get you both back on the track of enjoying each other's company.

+ Ensure that the young person wins. It is so easy to use our superior size and power to win at games we play with our children and stepchildren - at last we have the chance to win when perhaps we never won when we were young ourselves. But that can really feel discouraging to children and young people, it is more useful to put up stiff resistance and allow them to win in the end. Of course, this is not necessary when the children are older and bigger and can beat us in the games that we play together.

In Chapter 6 we look at listening. One of the listening styles that we introduce is called reflective listening. You can think of the suggestions outlined above as a kind of reflective listening through play which has been called 'play-listening'.

A special place

Make a special 'private' place for each person in the household - both adults and young people, and those who live there and those who do not. It is best to include everybody in plans to arrange this so that everybody's wishes are accommodated as much as is possible.

We all need a space that we can call our own. This may just be a drawer or a shelf in a cupboard for children who come to visit at weekends. Where children have to share a room it can be helpful if particular parts of the room belong to each child for them to use as they wish. Thus there may be a desk or a cupboard for each child to use just for their own things.

For such a system to work, property rights need to be respected:

- The owner of each space has control over that space. Nobody else may intrude without the owner's express permission.
- People are free to do what they want with their space. It must not be taken over for storing things that do not belong to the owner.
- You will need to ensure that the space created for a non-resident child is respected as theirs at all times, both when they are in the home and when they are not.
- If a whole room is available to a person, that space needs to be respected in the same way as the more limited spaces discussed above.

Summary

In this section we have discussed the importance of building relationships with our children and stepchildren. We have considered the complexity of stepfamily relationships and the difficulty of juggling time in such a way that everybody's needs can be met in the limited time available. We have introduced the concepts of values, special time and the need for everybody to have their own space for their special possessions.

Notes to myself on what I have learned

6

Listening skills

"Mike tried to show he loved her by buying her presents but she just got angry and often smashed them. She just kept saying 'I don't want them from you, I want them from my Dad'."

"When Lucy told me how frightened she was that she'd never see her Dad again I realised how jealous I had been of her. It's taken several years but I think we're friends now."

Helpful and unhelpful listening

When somebody comes to us because they are feeling upset, it is very easy for us to go into problem solving mode and offer them a solution. There are a number of problems with this approach:

+ the person with the problem does not learn how to solve their own problem
+ the person with the problem becomes dependent on others to solve their problem
+ our solution may work for us but it may not work for the other person.

In many situations it is more useful to listen to the other person talking about their feelings, to respond in a way that shows that we care and to act as a kind of sounding board for them to get their feelings off their chest. We usually experience the person who says very little but gives us the feeling that they understand how we feel as a helpful listener.

But what is it that such a person does? What are the qualities of a helpful listener?

Qualities of a helpful listener

A helpful listener essentially listens to a person who is feeling upset, or has a difficulty which they cannot solve, in such a way that they are able to sort out the situation for themselves.

A helpful listener:

*   has a non-judgmental attitude and communicates **acceptance** of the talker's feelings
*   **cares** about the person enough to want to help them to solve their own problem
*   takes the time to try to **understand** how the other person feels
*   **trusts** that the person with the problem can find their own solution.

In this section we are focusing on listening to our children and stepchildren, but everything that is written here can be applied to anybody we are listening to.

Acceptance

It is not as easy as it may seem to be accepting of another person's feelings. And it can be especially difficult to be accepting of our children's and stepchildren's feelings. Our hopes, our expectations and our wishes for our children can be so strong that it can be hard to put them aside and see our children as beings who are separate from us with lives of their own.

In an earlier section we talked about acknowledging feelings. When our children tell us something they are upset about -

especially if it is something about us - it is easy to get defensive or argue with the content of what they are saying. Instead we can acknowledge that they feel that way without getting drawn into a discussion of the content of what they are saying. So if our stepchild says to us: "I don't like the way you always tell me what to do", we could respond by saying: "You don't like me using that tone of voice". A child is likely to feel heard by such an acknowledgement whereas "Don't talk to me like that" is likely to lead to an argument and bad feeling.

Caring

It is generally much quicker to solve your child's problem than to support them to solve it themselves. By taking the time to listen to their upset feelings and ask them questions that help them see the situation in a new light we show them that we care about them. If we jump in to solve their problem, we may be communicating to them that we don't care enough to let them learn in their own time from any mistakes they may make.

Understanding

As adults it is easy to think that we know best and to forget that the world often looks different through a child's eyes. It is important to take the time to try and see the world through your children's eyes, to try and put yourself into their shoes.

So often, tensions between parents and children come from two completely different perceptions of the same situation.

The mother of a three-year-old told how she had opened the front door to find the paper and three bottles of milk on the step and said "Drat! I only wanted two." She picked up the paper and two of the

*bottles to carry them through to the kitchen. As she
returned for the third bottle she heard the crash of
broken glass and saw her daughter leaning over the
gate looking at the broken milk bottle she had just
thrown on the pavement. "What on earth are you
doing?" she called out angrily, and as the child turned
she saw her face change from innocent satisfaction to
shock and horror. Anger, defiance and distress
mingled as the child cried "But you said you didn't
want the other one".* (Taken from *Play is a Feeling* by
Brenda Crowe)

Understanding the other perspective can help us be more
accepting of our children.

Trust

We need to have the confidence that our children are able to
resolve their own problems. And we need to express that
confidence in them. The more we are able to trust them to
help themselves, and turn to us for assistance when they need
it, the more they will be able to trust themselves to be in
charge of their lives and learn from their mistakes as they
make them.

Our own childhoods

Our own experience as children has a great influence on the
kind of people that we are and greatly affects the way we
parent our children, whether we are aware of it or not. It is
widely recognised that the abused child may become an
abusing parent. It is also the case that the child who received
affection is likely to become an affectionate parent and the
criticised child a critical parent, and so on. These 'inherited'
patterns of behaviour seem to permeate almost everything we
do as parents.

It is useful to spend time talking with others about our own childhood experiences in order to see how they affect us in the present. If you have joined a Learning to Step Together group you will at times have the opportunity to talk with others about memories from your childhood. However, you may also like to fix a time with your partner or a friend to explore your childhood and notice any patterns of behaviour which you think may be influencing the kind of parent or step-parent you are. The first step toward changing any patterns of behaviour is becoming aware of them.

Listening partnerships

Some parents have set up 'listening partnerships' along the following lines: one person talks first and the other person listens and asks questions of the talker to draw out details of their story. Then the two switch roles and the first listener becomes the talker and talks to the first talker who is now the listener. The advantage of such a format is that it means that each person has the chance to talk about their own experience without interruption. You may also find it useful to agree how long you will talk and to ensure that you share time equally. Some people find it easier to talk and others find it easier to listen. However, we all need to talk and reflect on our own experiences - as well as listening to others doing the same - and dividing time equally ensures that we each have the opportunity to do both.

Body language

The US anthropologist, Dr. Ray Birdwhistel, who coined the phrase 'body language' analysed interactions between people in pairs and in small groups to discover how much of our communication was non-verbal. He came up with the following surprising statistics:

Words	*Less than 1/5*	(7%)
Tone of voice	*About 1/4*	(23%)
Facial expression	*More than 1/3*	(35%)
Gestures	*More than 1/3*	(35%)

What this shows is that the vast majority of our communication takes place at a non-verbal level. We take more notice of facial expressions and gestures than the words people use, and it is the tone of voice conveying the words which is more important than what is actually being said.

For example: if your child returns to the stepfamily home after visiting his other parent and in response to your question about his day says "It was alright" with a gruff expression and a miserable looking face, you would know that it wasn't really alright and that he wasn't saying how he actually felt.

As adults we tend to put our attention on the content (that is, the words) of what people say. We are generally not aware of the non-verbal communication though it still affects us. How would you feel if you have something of great importance to say to another person and they are standing up, looking as though they could walk off at any minute? You would probably feel that they have little time for you and you may not bother talking about what is actually on your mind. You may not be conscious of why you do not talk but you may have a nagging sense of being ignored.

It is not enough to focus on words. When we are in good rapport with another person, our non-verbal communication tends to instinctively 'match' theirs: if they sit, we will sit; if they talk quietly, we are likely to talk quietly; we may even adopt similar postures such as both of us leaning slightly forwards or sitting straight with arms crossed. We communicate empathy with our bodies as well as our words.

On an intuitive level our children tend to be much more conscious of body language. There are a number of ways in which we can raise our awareness of non-verbal communication in order to create better rapport with our children.

- When listening to our children, or when talking about important matters, we can ensure that we are both on the same level. We can either lift them up to our height by perhaps sitting them on a table or work surface, or we can crouch down at their level. In this way we are 'matching' their height.
- When our children are talking to us we can stop whatever we are doing and give them our full attention. Children sometimes take their time to tell us what is in their minds. If we go straight back to what we were doing we are communicating that we are not really listening, whether we are or not.
- Often we speak louder and more quickly than our children. If we speak more quietly and slowly, thus matching them in pace and volume, then they are more likely to feel that we are 'with' them.
- We can pay attention to our children's body language. Children communicate in unspoken ways just as much as adults do. We can acknowledge our children's unspoken feelings.
- Children may stomp around making angry noises or complain and be miserable when they are feeling fed up. We can playfully join in with them, matching and following their noises and movements. As we get into rapport with them the tension may break and they (and we) may fall about laughing.

Giving clear messages

If a child is running around with a pencil in their mouth we may say: "I'm scared that if you run around like that, you may fall and hurt yourself." If we do not express the extent of our fear, they may not take any notice of us. Similarly, we may quietly say "I am so angry" through clenched teeth, without communicating the full force of our anger. We are giving mixed messages. This is called being 'incongruent'.

If our words and actions do not match and are incongruent, they are likely to confuse our children and our words will have limited effect. Remembering that our children are particularly aware of our non-verbal communication, we need to ensure that our whole bodies communicate what our words say. Very often our children will ignore our words when we are being incongruent. We will get more and more frustrated until we really say (or shout) what we mean and then they are more likely to respond as our tone, expression and gestures match our words. In this way our children often 'force' us to be congruent.

Different ways of listening

Silent listening

Although we may not be aware of it, we tend to interrupt other people when they are talking, or be interrupted ourselves when we are talking. As a result, the experience of being listened to silently without interruption can be very powerful. We often underestimate the power of listening but, in fact, just being listened to by another person makes a big difference. Here is a story from one of the Parent Network booklets that accompany their Parent-Link education and support programme (see resource list):

My 13-year-old daughter came home from school one day obviously upset. She threw her schoolbag on the floor in the hall, stamped through the kitchen and out of the back door. I got up and followed her out, finding her sitting on the back steps. I sensed her feeling hurt and upset and close to tears. I sat down beside her to listen if she wanted to talk. I imagined sending love waves to her so she would know I was there to help if she needed me. After 10 minutes she sighed a huge sigh, stood up and stretched and said: "Thanks for listening mum," before going inside obviously feeling better.

For many children struggling to make sense of the changes in their family life, their parent's death or their parents' separation, and the presence of a step-parent, this silent reassuring listening may be of enormous value.

Asking questions

Once we have learnt to bite our tongue and actually listen to our children - and it is surprisingly difficult to *really* listen - there are certain ways of asking questions that are likely to encourage your children to talk about what they have been doing and how they are feeling. There are other ways which are likely to get one word answers and leave control of the conversation with you, or to cause them to 'dry up'.

Closed questions

A closed question is one that leads to the answer 'yes' or 'no'. They are asked to obtain a piece of information for the questioner but are rarely helpful to the talker. And a closed question gets a one word answer and leaves the conversation with the questioner.

Examples of closed questions:
+ Did you enjoy school today?
+ Did you enjoy your trip to Daddy's house?
+ Was Jamie horrible to you again?

Open-ended questions
This type of question gives the other person the space to
answer as he or she wishes and does not limit their answer in
any way.

Examples of open-ended questions are:
+ What did you do at school?
+ How did you spend your time at Daddy's?
+ What did you and Jamie play?

People who are considered to be helpful listeners rarely ask
questions. But if they do, they tend to ask open-ended
questions which invite the speaker to say more about their
feelings or concerns. But remember, the purpose of asking
questions is to help the talker on his or her journey. Here are
some examples of *un*-helpful reasons for asking questions:
+ to satisfy your own curiosity
+ to fill uncomfortable silences
+ to hide a statement. So "Why are you making so much
  noise?" could be hiding the statement: "Right now I want
  peace and quiet". It is usually better to say what you
  want than to hide it with a question.

Reflective listening
In reflective listening, the listener reflects back to the other
person what they understand them to be communicating. For
example, we might say: "You look sad" to a child with a
forlorn look rather than "What's the matter?" This gives the

child-talker a feeling of being really listened to and accepted. "What's the matter?" can feel like an intrusion, especially if your child is not sure they are ready to talk about their feelings.

Very often a simple 'reflection' of what we see and hear is enough of an invitation for the other person to be able to share their feelings with us, and we can continue to reflect back the content of what is being said until the talker has finished. If we give the other person the chance to express their fears, problems can resolve themselves as if by magic. Ordinary questions may be experienced as an interrogation and lead to silence whereas descriptive statements of what you see and hear can help open a locked door.

Reflective listening is particularly useful in a number of different situations:

When people are overcome by strong feelings. Reflecting back how they seem to be feeling often helps them 'discharge' these feelings until they feel calmer again. Remember about the healing power of tears (see p40 in the session 'The new stepfamily') and the importance of listening to people who are 'emotionally flooded'. Reflective listening is most useful in such situations. However we need to have learnt to feel at ease with other people's deeper emotions. Our reflections of other people's feelings need to show that we understand how the other person is feeling and feel relaxed with their distress. For example, it can be very painful to hear our child say something like "I hate being in this family. I wish you and Daddy had never divorced. I wish you had never met Alan." It may be so painful to us that we cannot respond empathically to their pain. In this case we need to find someone to listen to our feelings (perhaps in a listening partnership as described above) to help us come to terms with the feelings it brings up in us before we will be able to respond to our child in a relaxed and supportive way. Then we might reflect back to them: "It must really hurt to feel like that."

It can help people with their thinking, when they are trying to think through a difficult situation or develop some new ideas. Hearing your ideas fed back to you by another person can help you clarify them, as a result of 'hearing' them through somebody else's eyes.

In essence what you are doing when you use reflective listening is:
+ feeding back the content of what the person is saying
+ feeding back the feelings behind what they are saying.

The effect of reflective listening on the talker is to:
+ increase self-esteem by leaving them with the responsibility
+ giving them a feeling of being accepted.

Problems are like onions. In reflecting back the 'presenting problem', people will often uncover a deeper problem. Questions directed at the 'presenting problem' will often prevent the talker from finding out what lies underneath. We often do not know why we are feeling the things we are feeling. Reflective listening helps us find out why.

When not to be a listener

Parents (like children) are only human! You cannot always listen to your children when they want your attention. Such times might be:
+ When you are too tired to listen and you just haven't got

the energy. Rather than pretending to listen - which your children are likely to see through anyway, you could say something along the following lines: "Right now I'm too tired to listen to you telling me about your day. I'd really like to hear when I'm feeling up to it - perhaps after tea." This acknowledges how you are feeling and shows your child that you care about them.

♦ When you are in emotional turmoil and you do not have the calmness or detachment to listen to your children in a useful way. Such times might be when you are going through a divorce or separation or when you are in the process of forming a new stepfamily. At such times it will really help your children (and you) if there is at least one other adult - maybe a member of your wider family or a close family friend - who can be available to support your children when they need it.

Rather than blaming yourself for not always being there for your children, you can look at it this way:

♦ By looking after your own needs, you are modelling to your children an important lesson: our feelings are important and we need to look after ourselves. Looking after ourselves enables us to joyfully care for and look after others.

♦ By telling our children how we are feeling we are modelling to them that it is important to acknowledge and express our feelings.

Summary

In this section we have discussed the importance of listening to children. We have talked about the importance of giving clear messages and the value in remembering that we communicate with our whole bodies and not just with our words. We have talked about silent listening, open-ended questions and reflective listening and perhaps, most important of all, we have talked about the times when not to listen.

Parents need to be listened to as well, a fact that is forgotten by most people. We can only listen to our children well if we have people who listen to us. By ensuring that you get the time you need from your partner and your friends, you are doing both yourself and your children a service.

Notes to myself on what I have learned

7

Setting rules

"It's no good expecting them to accept the new rules you want. They'd been used to staying up late keeping their Mum company and were very angry when I wanted us to have some time in the evening on our own."

"Some weekends we've got seven children here. My two, his three staying over and the two little ones. If we didn't all sit down together and work out who was doing what it would be a madhouse."

Discipline in the stepfamily home

The use of discipline by a step-parent needs to proceed slowly on the basis of developing a sense of respect and caring between the stepchild and step-parent, and also on the basis of trust between the two adults and child. If the step-parent moves too quickly, the parent may undermine the disciplining process by perceiving the discipline as too severe. Intervention by the parent may then cause the step-parent to withdraw completely from disciplining. That in turn can cause tension between the couple. While the step-parent moves slowly towards a more authoritative relationship from friendship and affection, the parent needs to be the initial 'rule enforcer', but from the early stages the couple needs to work together on what the rules of the household are to be.

The parent also moves through a major change in the home and with the children, and needs time to do this. He or she

111

must get used to sharing the decision-making with another adult after being a lone-parent household. This is something which individuals and couples vary about in terms of the time needed to make the transition from acting independently to acting together in planning and deciding how the family will run, what behaviour is allowed, and so on. Children may also resent the change in the early stages because in the single-parent household they may have had more influence.

Ideally, everyone needs to be involved in the decision-making process in order for discipline to be effective. Adults must take responsibility for making the final decisions, but children need to be heard too.

Rules

Rules for children need to be clearly defined, reasonable and enforceable. A rule needs to be stated in terms of behaviour, with a specific description of expectations. A reasonable rule is one that can be understood by a child, and one that is within the child's physical capabilities to carry out. For a rule to be enforceable, there needs to be:

♦ a set time limit,
♦ a specific desired behaviour,
♦ and an adult present to observe it.

Rules work best when they are stated briefly and in positive terms. For example,
"When you pick up your toys you may watch TV", or
"When you finish the washing up, you can have some pudding".

The statements above are preferable to:
"If you don't pick up your toys, you may not watch TV", or

"You can't have any pudding unless you finish the washing up".

Those statements are negative, they are threats and do not create a desire in the child to be helpful or co-operative.

When deciding upon appropriate discipline for a child, it is important that the punishment reinforces the desired behaviour and is acceptable to the adults. It does not make sense to set a punishment for a child that you are unwilling or unable to enforce or that you feel is too harsh. Also, it is not useful to offer something the child doesn't really want. For example, if you ask a child to clean up their room so that they can go to the park, that will only act as a reinforcement if they actually want to go to the park.

Contingency rules

To teach a child to carry out responsibilities, requires the less preferred activity to come before a more preferred activity (fun).

Activities a child likes to do can be used to *reinforce* doing things a child cares less about.

Examples:

"When you finish your homework you can go out."

"Eat your vegetables and then you can have some pudding."

"When your room is cleared up, I've got a special treat for you."

"Take your bath and then you can have some biscuits."

"After you have taken out the rubbish, you can go out to play."

Instead of:

> "You can go out and play if you'll do your homework later."

> "You can watch a video tonight, if you'll do your homework tomorrow."

Setting rules: changing behaviour

Step by Step

For a rule to work, it must be definable, reasonable and enforceable.

Definable means parents must be specific about what they want the child to do.

Reasonable means the rule must be within the child's physical and mental capabilities.

Enforceable means a parent must be able to enforce a rule consistently.

1. Select one behaviour on which to focus. It is desirable to concentrate on only *one behaviour* at a time.

_____

_____

2. Describe the behaviour you consider undesirable, in very specific terms. To change a behaviour, it is most helpful if what you wish to change is clearly specified (so clearly that an observer would know for certain that the behaviour is or is

not occurring - specific time of day, exact words, specific actions).

_____

_____

_____

3. Describe the actual behaviour you wish to establish.

_____

_____

_____

4. Since behaviour does not change all at once, list the change in reasonable steps (if this applies).

a. _____

b. _____

c. _____

d. _____

5. Check if the behaviour you want to establish fits the definitions we have discussed.

Definable_____ Reasonable_____ Enforceable_____

6. Does the person whose behaviour you wish to change know what behaviours you consider acceptable?

_____

How do you plan to let them know?

_____

a. Consequences or rewards for acceptable behaviour.

_____

b. Consequences or restrictions for unacceptable behaviour.

_____

7. State the rule as you will present it to your child.

_____

_____

_____

Family meetings

Family meetings help a stepfamily open up communication and begin to share the business of living together. Family meetings can also solve, or begin to solve, practical problems by giving everyone a chance to be heard, by distributing chores among family members, expressing concerns and complaints, expressing good feelings and giving encouragement, settling conflicts that keep arising and planning family outings.

Family meetings work best when there is a conscious decision to work together. Partners need to be supportive of each other during this process. Couples in stepfamilies may vary as to when they are able to support each other in this way especially if they have not spent adequate time on their own working out how they want the new stepfamily to work. Both need to feel that their point of view is valuable. Children of any age can be acutely aware of differences between a parent and step-parent or between both their birth parents. They will also be looking closely at your reactions to see whether or not their suggestions and feelings are taken seriously, and whether or not they are really being listened to. The family meeting provides an opportunity for children to develop assertiveness, and the more their rights are respected the more they will learn to respect other family members' rights. The self-respect they learn will help them outside the family as well as in it.

When children are encouraged to generate ideas for solutions to problems, they are more able to take responsibility for changes in the family and work co-operatively with their parent and step-parent, while at the same time learning that the parents are fair in setting the final, safe limits.

Here is an example of how a parent may set a framework for action while enabling their child to generate the ideas to solve a problem:

> *John did not want to have contact with his father, who lives apart from him, because he did not enjoy the visits. His mother knew that it was important for John to*

continue to stay in touch, so she wanted John to continue visiting his father. Rather than forcing John to visit his father, John's mother decided to help him explore the reasons why he did not like the visits and find ways of changing the visits so that he does enjoy them. John's mother can also encourage him to discuss this with his father or, with John's agreement, his mother can contact his father and suggest some of the changes John has identified. (Supporting a child in this way can be particularly difficult if there are still tensions between the separated parents. However, for your child's sake you need to find a way of putting aside such feelings.)

We know from experience that stepchildren can be just as proud of their stepfamilies as are children growing up with both their birth parents. Living in a stepfamily provides new opportunities for children to:

+ raise their awareness of the differences between people and families and recognise that such differences aren't necessarily 'better' or 'worse' but are just reflections of different values and approaches to life
+ develop communication and negotiation skills to manage these differences in values.

Guidelines for family meetings

1. Meet at a regular scheduled time and be consistent.
2. Rotate the responsibility for leading the meeting among all family members.
3. Plan a specific amount of time to meet, twenty or thirty minutes, depending on the ages of the children and the number of items to be discussed.
4. All family members need to have an opportunity to make suggestions. Adults need to be careful not to dominate with an agenda or with solutions to problems.
5. Meetings are not productive if they become merely moan sessions. Encourage family members to share positive things that have happened to them during the week, and to say what they are enjoying about each other. Encourage compliments and support for each other as well as discussion of complaints.
6. To decide household chores, have everyone make a list and discuss how to distribute tasks fairly.
7. Agreements stay in effect until the next family meeting, when they can be renegotiated if necessary.
8. Complaints need to be discussed with everyone present.
9. The family meeting provides an opportunity for everyone to bring up issues, not just adults. Keeping an agenda can ensure that everyone has been encouraged to raise issues during the family meetings.
10. Make the meetings more than problem-solving sessions. Ideally, they need to include fun items, such as planning for family outings, leisure activities or celebrations.
11. Meetings can also be a time when different parts of the family learn about each other's history, and the changes can be discussed in a matter-of-fact way.

Whose problem is it?

Many problems that occur when we live together in families can be dealt with more easily if we are familiar with the concept of 'problem ownership'. Problem ownership enables us to stand back and decide:

+ "Who has a problem?" and
+ "Whose needs need meeting first?"

If a child is upset - because his needs are not being met or are being interfered with by others, he has got a problem.

Examples of situations in which the child owns the problem are:

+ John is annoyed because he cannot find his toy.
+ Jenny is scared because she has been bullied by some bigger girls at school.
+ Marlene is feeling lonely because nobody will play with her.
+ Henry is angry because his stepfather is always telling him what to do.

Similarly, the parent may be upset by their child or stepchild's behaviour:

Examples of situations in which the parent owns the problem are:

+ Richard is irritated because the children keep interrupting him while he is talking on the telephone.
+ Leah is annoyed because the children have splashed water all over the floor.
+ George is angry because the children are making a noise when he has asked for quiet because of his headache.
+ Isobel feels sad because her stepdaughter refuses to talk to her.

In many situations both parents and children own part of the problem.

So, for example:

1. When John is annoyed because he can't find his toy, his stepfather feels annoyed too because he is continually telling his wife that John is old enough to be taught to put his things away safely - to no avail.
2. When Jenny tells her mother that she is being bullied at school, her mother is both angry about the bullying and worried for Jenny's safety.
3. Marlene's stepmother feels worried about Marlene because she doesn't have any friends to play with when she is staying every other weekend and during school holidays.

As parents and step-parents we often become emotionally involved in our children's and stepchildren's problems - as in the above examples - and then we may either take on the problem and try and solve it (as if it were our own) or, because of our upset feelings, we are not able to think straight and help our child with their problem.

Often we are so close to our children it is hard to know where we end and where they begin. When our children feel upset we may automatically take action to alleviate their upset without really being aware of what we are doing. It's as if we feel our children's feelings - as if they were our own - and then instinctively act on them rather than standing back, taking stock of the situation and then deciding what to do. Asking ourselves the question "Whose problem is it?" enables us to look at the situation and decide who owns the problem and who is best placed to try and resolve it. If we decide that more than one person owns the problem then we can ask ourselves a second question: "Whose needs need meeting first?"

Let's analyse the above examples a little further:

1. When John's stepfather asks himself whose needs need meeting first, he decides that John's do. He decides to put aside his own annoyance, acknowledge his stepson's frustration and help him think about ensuring he doesn't lose things in future.

2. Jenny's mother is so upset about the bullying that she decides she has to talk it over with a friend before sitting down with Jenny to work out with her what needs to be done. In this case Jenny's mother has decided that her needs need meeting first. When she has calmed down she will be able to usefully help Jenny.

3. Marlene's stepmother decides to put aside her worries about Marlene's loneliness and she sits down with her stepdaughter to help her think how she wants to spend her time when she is visiting and whether she actually wants to make some local friends.

When parents take on their children's problems and try to solve them themselves they disempower their children by preventing them from learning to be responsible for themselves. If we constantly look for our children's toys when they are lost, then our children may not learn how to look after their own things. If, when our child is being bullied at school, we go straight down to school to sort it out without discussing the situation with our child, then she may learn that she needs her parents to sort out her problems. By enabling our children to sort out their own problems and giving them whatever kind of assistance they need, we are helping them on the path to independence.

When our children own the problem we can use our helping

and listening skills (as discussed in the section Listening skills on p96). When we own the problem we need to decide whether to deal with our own feelings or challenge our children in order to get them to change their behaviour.

As children grow up

When children reach adolescence many parents and step-parents are confronted with a particular difficulty which may not have been so obvious when their children were younger. Suddenly their children appear to become more defiant, refuse to fit in with the family or 'do as they are asked'. Any issue may be the focus of such flash points but rows commonly focus on: staying out late, untidy bedrooms, rudeness, money, parents wanting to know where they are going and with whom, and young people resenting parental 'interference' and the demands made on their time to spend time with both parents rather than with their friends.

Parents often do not know how to deal with such situations. They may experience such behaviour as challenges to their authority, when in the past their child would have been happy to go along with their request. Arguments may ensue in which both sides (parents and adolescents) blame the other for their behaviour. 'You' messages are thrown back and forth and real communication and understanding does not take place. Instead, lingering anger, frustration and resentment may be felt by both sides.

Asking yourself who owns the problem can help you, the parent, know how to respond. When you are beset by concerns for your child or feel angered by your child's behaviour, then you, the parent, own the problem. When you own the problem there are two alternative responses which may lead to an effective resolution of your problem:

- ***To recognise that you need to hold back your feelings and work them out for yourself.*** For example, if you get annoyed at your child's untidy room you may decide that it is your problem because they have the right to have their room the way they want it. At the same time you may want to negotiate and come to an agreement, say, that their dirty clothes will be washed if they are put in the washing basket.

  Thus you might say: "I feel irritated that your room is so untidy but your room is your own. If you want me to wash your dirty clothes we are going to have to come to some arrangement as I'm not prepared to hunt through your room for them." However, there may also be a ground rule that food must never be allowed to accumulate and rot because you do not want to end up with mice or rats in the house.

- ***To express your feelings and challenge your child's behaviour with the aim of negotiating a solution.*** For example, you may wish to tell your child about your concerns for her safety when she stays out late, with a view to negotiating a solution that satisfies both you and her.

  Thus you may say: "When you stay out past the agreed time I worry that something might have happened to you. What can you do to help me?" Ensuring that they have a phone card or change for a telephone call box makes it possible for them to tell you if they are going to be late and how they are going to get home, as well as when they will arrive.

When young people reach adolescence they are taking on a

greater responsibility for their own lives. They are demanding more control over their lives and it can be difficult for parents to make the transition with them and learn to stand back and allow them to be in charge of their lives (and learn from their successes and mistakes) while at the same time being available and supportive to their children when they are needed.

Problem solving

Here is a simple problem-solving method for resolving conflict which could be used at a family meeting. This kind of negotiation can strengthen relationships within the family, whereas trying to bury or ignore conflict may create tensions, resentments and unhappiness.

1. State the problem (which may look different to different people).

2. Search for alternatives - 'brainstorming'. Everyone is encouraged to participate.

3. Identify the consequences of the alternatives.

4. Rank the alternatives in terms of desirability and feasibility.

5. Choose an alternative and commit the family to that solution.

Clear communication and challenging 'I' messages

Communication is probably the most important factor in determining what kinds of relationships a person forms with others, and in developing self-worth. All communication is learned. Good communication can be defined as 'creating understanding'. If feelings and thoughts are directly communicated without fear of reprisal, the family system can work well. If communication is indirect, squelched or vague, resentment arises and the family may deteriorate or break down.

Communication is both verbal and non-verbal. Non-verbal communication includes the messages conveyed by body posture, eye contact, facial expression and hand gestures. Verbal communication is what is said and how it is said. The combination of what we say and our expressions and gestures and how we use words, will provide a model for the way in which members of our stepfamily interact with us. At times words are the least important means of communication, and that is when the tone of voice and expression belie the words. Good communication will happen when the words, expression and body language agree (for a fuller discussion of verbal and non-verbal communication see the section entitled 'Body language' on p100).

Good communication is direct communication, and that means being assertive. Assertiveness training teaches people to stand up for their own rights without undermining the rights of others. Another way of doing this is to use challenging 'I' statements ('I' statements or 'I' messages were introduced in the section entitled 'Owning our feelings' on p67).

An 'I' statement involves four parts. It begins with what the person is feeling and then what the other person is doing or not doing to contribute to that feeling. The third part of the statement is the actual effect that the behaviour has on you and the fourth part includes a specific statement of what you would like or a request for suggestions from the other person.

For example, a step-parent may say to a stepchild, "**I feel** hurt **when you** come home from school and don't say hello **because** I am being ignored. **I would like** you to say hello when you come in". That sort of statement is clear and direct and is a model for the child of taking responsibility for their own feelings. It is more useful than the statement which asks "Why?" "Why don't you say hello when you come in from school?" is unlikely to encourage greater understanding or to result in a change of behaviour for example.

Commonly used 'You' messages often put people on the defensive and create barriers to communication. A 'You' message, such as the one in the example above, says something about the other person and tends to be judgmental. In contrast, an 'I' message is an explanation and a self disclosure. Using such statements will encourage the children to act in a similar way which will provide more opportunities to understand what children are feeling, and will encourage them to take responsibility for expressing their feelings without blaming parents and step-parents.

There is a simple formula for 'I' statements:

1. Stating your feeling. (**I feel ...**).

2. Stating the behaviour which makes you feel that way (**when you ...**).

3. Stating the actual effect (**because ...**).

4. Asking for help or making clear what it is you want. (**"What ideas do you have?"** or **"I would like you to .."**).

Here is one more example of this:

"**I feel** annoyed about your untidy room **because** I can never find your dirty clothes under the piles of things on the floor **when** I am trying to do a wash. **What suggestions do you have?**"

Saying no and sticking to it.

In the above section we have been discussing challenging and negotiating with our children in order to effect a change in their behaviour - and sometimes as a result we will change our behaviour too. However, there are some situations where it is not appropriate to negotiate. For example, in situations of danger or where a child's health is at risk.

Some parents find it hard to say 'no' to their children. They may (unconsciously) feel the pain of being told 'no' by their own parents and carers and they feel mean saying 'no' to their own children. But children need adults to set limits and they will often force us into situations where we have to say 'no' to them.

What is not helpful is to punish children for being upset by our 'no'. The pain that stays with the child over time is the pain that comes from the punishment, not the pain of being told 'no'.

And parents have the right to say 'no' at any time. Some parents feel that they have to give in to their children's every reasonable demand. But parents are only human. We have each got only a certain amount of time and energy that we can give to our children. Parents, especially mothers, often feel under pressure to constantly put their children first and themselves second. But our children need to see us looking after ourselves as well as looking after them. So it's alright to say 'no' to a child's reasonable request. What children need is an explanation. So we might say: "I know you really want me to play another game, but right now I haven't got the energy." Children need to know that there is a logic in the way we treat them. It is harsh and erratic discipline that confuses and damages them.

If we repeatedly say 'yes' when we actually feel 'no', then we are likely to end up feeling resentful. And our children may feel guilty for being a burden to us. Much better to say 'no', have an argument about it, clear the air and feel close again.

Much of the time when we say 'no' our children get upset. We repeat our 'no' louder and louder until we end up screaming and shouting and our children are in tears. Here are some alternative ideas:

+ Check with yourself that you really do mean 'no'. We often say 'no' before we have thought out our reasons properly. You could try saying: "Let me think about it. I'll give you an answer in a moment" to give you the time to think whether you really mean 'no'. It's better to say 'no' and mean it rather than changing your mind once you have said 'no'. That confuses children. And of course, there are times when we really need to change our mind - and that's OK too.

+ When you say 'no' to a child and they get upset, remember that you can acknowledge their upset and stay with 'no'. You can say things such as "You seem really disappointed that you can't have that last biscuit but I've said 'no' and I mean it". You can comfort the child through his or her distress while sticking with 'no'. This is a great help to children. If they are allowed to cry out all their disappointments and frustrations as they arise, anger and resentment won't build up inside them.

We need to remember as adults that many children find 'no' hard to accept. The disappointment of not being able to have what they want may feel to them as if their whole world has been destroyed. However, they need to learn to accept 'no'. We can best help them to do that by sticking with 'no' and allowing them to express their upset without punishing them for it. It can take many years for a young child to learn to come to terms with 'no'. Be patient with your children. And if you think about it, how many adults like being told 'no'. It hurts us too.

Summary

In this section we have discussed setting rules, family meetings, problem solving, whose problem is it, challenging 'I' messages and saying 'no'. These skills take practice and can help to improve communication and the practice of effective discipline in a stepfamily. Try to find opportunities to practise these skills, but before you do this, explain to your children and stepchildren, that you have learned something that you hope will encourage everyone to be more direct with each other.

Notes to myself on what I have learned

8

Strengthening the stepcouple relationship

"I know that it was best in the end for Sue and me to split. The kids did find it hard but now they've got two families that care about them and four lots of grandparents so it's worked out alright really. Sometimes they're still sad but they can see we are both happy."

"My Mum looks really good these days. She used to cry and drink and be so awful. With Ted she laughs, and we do things like go bowling. And my Dad's got a job and a new baby and he's not so angry anymore."

"When Fran died I could never imagine marrying again. We had a good marriage and two lovely kids - all shattered by her illness. Claire has shown me another way of being close and of being a family. She hasn't tried to replace Fran. She's a really special extra person to us all."

We've discussed the myths that affect stepfamilies, the structure of stepfamilies and the concerns of stepmothers, stepfathers and birth parents. We have also explored some of the feelings and concerns of stepchildren and have considered discipline, building self-esteem in children, rules and setting rules, family meetings and ways to improve communication. In this section we will concentrate on the importance of the unity and stability of the couple relationship. We will also discuss some of the topics frequently of concern to stepfamilies that could not be covered in the 'Learning to Step Together' course, such as legal and financial issues.

The couple

The key to family stability is the quality of the relationship between the adult partners as a couple. This bond is especially critical in stepfamilies and there are reasons for it being difficult to develop. It is essential that the couple in the stepfamily work out basic values and goals, and that they are clear about expectations and desires for their stepfamily. They each need to be patient with the other while those expectations become clear and realistic over time. The style and manner of the couple in doing these things sets the stage and tone for the way the rest of the family will act. Yet, because the adult couple in a stepfamily is the newest relationship in the family, it is often the most fragile and the most easily shaken. There may be financial stresses, struggles with strong parent/child bonds that were established before the couple existed, and conflicting loyalties to children and stepchildren.

The adults may be entering the new family with different emotional needs and different expectations of their responsibilities in the new household. It will take time to resolve these issues, but when a couple can communicate clearly, parenting and problem-solving will be improved.

Couples must allow themselves time to be alone, time to be intimate, and time to have fun together. There are many competing demands on the couples' time, including children and stepchildren, ex-partners, former relatives and daily demands of a job, homemaking and parenting. Adults will want time by themselves also, and time alone with their children. Time for friendships and outside activities is also important. All these competing interests need to be considered in the light of the essential need for the couple to have private time to enjoy closeness, resolve conflicts and build the foundation of a healthy relationship.

Good couple communication

There are several basic principles to sound couple communication:

☯ Set aside a certain amount of time each week to spend together. Have this time free from interruptions so that you have an opportunity to listen to each other.

☯ Use 'I' statements, and clear, direct messages about what you feel and want.

☯ Be aware of body language and body posture when communicating. Facing each other, making direct eye contact, and sitting with open body posture can help communication. That means, with head up, not slumped or closed by shoulders or legs turned away.

☯ Paraphrase when something seems vague to you. That is rephrase, in your own words what you think your partner has said and see if that is, in fact, what your partner means or is trying to say.

☯ Share emotions. Talking about your feelings is one of the most effective ways to build trust, openness and closeness in your relationship.

☯ Take the time to give positive and reinforcing feedback to each other by commenting on things that you like about each other, and openly appreciating what you do for each other. This builds closeness. Try to find something each day that your partner has done that you appreciate, that you enjoy, or that you respect, and share that with them.

☯ When conflicts arise, use the problem-solving model.

Support for Stepfamilies

Stepfamilies can benefit from a support network of other stepfamilies. Hopefully the series of meetings - from which you may have obtained this book - has provided everyone with an opportunity to meet members of other stepfamilies and develop a network that will continue beyond these meetings. Stepfamilies are often isolated. Members of stepfamilies often feel isolated in the family, and feel that their problems are unique and their stepfamily dilemmas are more difficult than most. Having a social network with other stepfamilies provides an opportunity to exchange ideas, and to share emotional support and resources. A social network can be important as a group to turn to in a crisis, but also encourages a continuing sharing of step-parenting skills - and strains.

There is an association for stepfamilies which can help to expand your network of contacts. This is the National STEPFAMILY Association. STEPFAMILY was founded by a stepmother who was feeling very isolated. STEPFAMILY now provides information for stepfamilies in all parts of the country. It runs a telephone counselling service and produces its own publications. Sometimes a family counsellor is needed to help a family with a very stuck problem. Such contacts are available from STEPFAMILY.

Legal issues

What are the responsibilities of a step-parent as defined by law? The status of the step-parent is not formally acknowledged by law. For example, the term step-parent is not used in the Children Act 1989. However, the step-parent is socially pressured to act in a protective role normally attributed to a parent. This role has usually been assumed voluntarily and may be stopped once the step-parent ceases to be in contact with the child should the marriage end.

Legal advisors have set out three general points:

1. Inheritance

As a general rule, if you are a step-parent or your partner is a step-parent to your children, you should take legal advice about making a Will so it is clear what you want to happen in the event of your death. The cost is generally not high and STEPFAMILY has produced a booklet to guide you on how to prepare to brief a solicitor as well as getting a quote for the job. It is not advisable to attempt to draw up a Will for yourself because stepfamilies are complex and it is extremely easy to make a mistake that causes complications which can be costly.

Stepchildren who have no blood relationship to you will not inherit under the rules which apply when a person has not made a Will. If you make a Will, your property, generally speaking, will pass to the people named by you as your 'beneficiaries'. It is important to remember that your children are stepchildren to your partner. If neither of you makes a Will, property can pass to a spouse and then to a spouse's own children, effectively missing out stepchildren in the process, unless they are specifically named or provided for.

Sometimes couples wish to ensure that their assets will only go to their children and not to their stepchildren. Resentments, hurt feelings and anger can occur as couples attempt to resolve these feelings to their satisfaction. Many parents feel a sense of financial obligation and duty to their children that they do not feel to their stepchildren. This is natural. However, the partner may regard this as lack of love or lack of commitment to the stepchildren. It is important to talk these things through.

Since many stepfamilies have 'his' and 'her' and 'their' children it is critical that you work through any anxieties and differences you may have. This issue needs to be clearly discussed as a couple, with each attempting to hear the concerns of the other. Since money is so often associated with commitment and attachment, it is easy for this to become a highly emotional issue which can drive a wedge between a couple. It obviously helps if you have seen a solicitor and worked out clearly the legal position for your family.

We do recommend you read the STEPFAMILY booklet on making a Will which offers different ways of resolving some of the common inheritance problems in stepfamilies, as well as the book on financial planning.

2. Parental Responsibility, Residence and other Related Issues

Where both parents of a child are alive, the involvement of each will depend to some extent on the arrangement between the two parents, and to some extent on the legal powers conferred by the Court. The 1989 Children Act (implemented in October 1991) has brought in several changes mentioned below and described in more detail in a STEPFAMILY book *Parenting Threads, Caring for children when couples part.* Previously, a Court made an order giving custody to one parent, or the other, or joint custody. If there was joint custody, the non-custodial parent had more of an automatic right to be consulted on all the major decisions for that child, such as education, medical treatment and religious upbringing. Even if the non-custodial parent did not have joint custody, he or she was entitled to intervene in the major decisions regarding the child and could, if such matters became disputed between the parents, take the matter back to Court for the Court's decision.

Whilst the step-parent may have had a highly influential role, he or she does not automatically have any legal right to intervene and make those decisions for the child.

Under the 1989 Children Act both named parents, if they were married, have continuing parental responsibility for their children. This replaces the previous concept of parental rights and duties. Parental responsibility means each has the right of independent action. An unmarried father can acquire parental responsibility but he will not have it automatically even if his name is on the birth certificate. After divorce this position holds, with both parents retaining equal decision-making power, unless a Residence Order is granted. These replace joint custody and custodianship orders.

The Act permits a step-parent who is married to a child's parent to acquire parental responsibility by applying for a Residence Order. Without a Residence Order a step-parent is in the same position as any other person who may be caring for a child without having parental responsibility. However, a parent may delegate power to a step-parent; for example to take a child to the Doctor. This should make it easier for stepfamilies to care for stepchildren in most everyday circumstances without undue enquiry and interference.

On the death of their spouse (the child's parent) the step-parent has no new rights automatically in relation to the stepchild but he or she may be appointed as the child's guardian. A Will or deed is no longer required; a signed, witnessed written document is sufficient. The appointment will not operate during the lifetime of the other parent unless the appointee is a step-parent with a Residence Order in his or her favour.

Adoption used to be seen as a way of giving step-parents a legal status in the family. Past restrictions on adoption by a parent and step-parent have been abolished by the 1989 Children Act. However, under the Act, the court will only make an order (including an adoption order) if it considers that this is better for the child than making *no* order. If the Court considers adoption is inappropriate, it may make a Residence Order instead.

If an adoption order is made, it legally ends the old family and the status of the children's birth parents and recognises the adoptive parents (usually mother and stepfather) as the children's only legal parents. An adoption certificate replaces the birth certificate and the children's family name may be changed. Adopted children inherit from their adoptive parents even if no Will is made.

Adoption orders usually require the agreement of the other birth parent although this may be dispensed with in extreme circumstances. There will also be a thorough investigation of the family circumstances by a social worker. In the past, adoption was sometimes used to conceal a child's past. This is no longer possible. The social worker will want to be sure that the child understands and accepts what is proposed. At the age of eighteen an adopted child has the right to his or her original birth certificate. Anyone contemplating adoption would be well advised to discuss it at length with a social worker and all concerned in the proceedings before making any decision.

New legislation following proposals in the Adoption Law Review undertaken in 1990 may introduce a new form of step-parent adoption and an alternative Parental Responsibility Agreement for married step-parents.

If you are thinking of ways to formalise your legal role as a step-parent then get hold of the STEPFAMILY leaflet entitled *Adopting Stepchildren* or consult your local solicitor or social services department. Legal advice is essential but unfortunately not all solicitors have experience with this type of work. We suggest you approach a solicitor who belongs to the Solicitors Family Law Association (see useful addresses).

3. Benefits
Financial planning in stepfamilies can be particularly complicated and can only be briefly mentioned here. A book on financial planning in stepfamilies is available from STEPFAMILY.

If a step-parent claims benefit, for example unemployment benefit or income support, an allowance will be included for each stepchild who is being maintained in the family. However, an adult step-child cannot claim housing benefit while living in the stepfamily, unless they had previously paid rent.

If a parent receives maintenance from their former spouse for a child this will be deducted from the benefit paid. The Department of Social Security takes the same approach even if the parent and step-parent have not actually married. However, if the parent and step-parent are separated there is no legal obligation under the Child Support Act 1991 for the step-parent to provide for the stepchild but he or she can be made to pay child support under a court order.

If a step-parent is left supporting a stepchild he or she may qualify for various allowances depending on financial and other circumstances.

If you are unsure about rights to, or deductions from, benefit you can consult your local C.A.B. or Welfare Rights Office.

Since April 1993 all child support assessments where the person looking after children is on benefit have been handled by the Child Support Agency. It is intended to phase in from April 1996 all new cases of child support, and any old cases previously dealt with in the courts will be required to seek child support through the Child Support Agency and no longer through the courts.

Finances

Money is often a source of friction in many families; however, in stepfamilies it is an especially sensitive and complex issue. Often finances are at the top of the list next to discipline in the problems cited by stepfamilies. The areas that often cause debate are: who earns the money, to whom is the money given, who pays for whose children and how is the money spent. Women may feel guilty about the financial burden they are placing on their new partners, and men may feel reluctant to accept and use as general funds the child support payments coming from their partner's ex-spouse.

There are also serious financial pressures on a parent or step-parent who is supporting two households. Such pressures may be even more acute now that the Child Support Act is implemented. Sometimes it is necessary for a woman to continue in paid work in order to help her partner to meet child support payments. It is not unusual for the woman in such a position to resent payments to the former wife or partner, although intellectually she knows that this commitment to his children must be met. This can be made much worse when there is little or no child support being received into the stepfamily for her children (his stepchildren) and the child support going out creates financial difficulties for the stepfamily. This is especially so where the couple have their own joint children. For many couples, money becomes an extremely sensitive subject that is difficult to discuss. It becomes an emotionally charged issue and may be seen as a measure of love or as a continuation of unresolved conflict between separated parents.

There is often conflict over how to use child support money. Should it be kept separate and used only for the children, or should it form part of the family income? In addition, men and women who have been handling money on their own for a number of years before the stepfamily, or who had stressful monetary conflicts at an earlier period, often find it difficult to be open about money, or to decide how to share. However, evidence suggests that the very experience of managing independently as a lone parent household is a good indicator of success for a woman in a stepfamily. A woman is more able to negotiate on money matters and other areas when she has managed alone, however difficult that may have been.

Communication between the couple is essential on money issues, as in other areas. Often neither wants to talk about money, but it is important for stepfamily couples to be realistic and honest about what their financial situation is, what their obligations are outside the family and what standard of living is possible for them to sustain. It is not uncommon for the stepfamily to have a lower standard of living than either adult was accustomed to in a prior family. Money issues must be dealt with early in the new family, often before either partner really wants to face up to such a subject, and possibly before they have learned to relate in a matter of fact way.

Financial exercise

Here is an exercise (taken from *His, Hers and Theirs: A Financial Handbook for Stepfamilies*) to stimulate thought and discussion about money issues in your family. You may like to reflect on the statements and your responses just for yourself and you may like to ask your partner and your children and stepchildren for their responses to some or all of the statements.

Tick which of the following statements most closely reflect your own beliefs and experiences about:

Growing up
(For 'my parents' you may wish to substitute 'the people who brought me up'.)
- My parents were extremely cautious, they only spent what they had.
- There were constant arguments about money.
- I was conscious of being different from other children because of my family's financial situation.
- Money was a taboo subject.
- My parents were very free and easy with their money, even if they got into debt.
- Money dominated our lifestyle.
- I vowed that financially I'd be very different from my parents.

The family and financial support

(Family in this context means parents, siblings and other blood relatives.)

- My family think it's up to me to sort myself out financially.
- There's no question my family would give whatever they could.
- I'd never dream of asking family or friends for help.
- I think it's my duty to stick by my family financially.
- I can't take financial responsibility for other people's mistakes.
- My family expects too much of me financially.

Your partner

- We pool all our resources and regard everything we own as belonging to us equally.
- As far as possible we each keep our financial affairs completely private.
- I leave all the financial dealings to my partner - I don't know what decisions have been taken.
- We talk everything through and usually agree on what to do.
- Every time we talk about money we end up rowing.
- We don't tend to discuss money, things just happen.
- My partner and I have very different attitudes towards money.
- I feel very protective towards 'my' money.

The impact of previous relationships

- My previous relationship has affected the way I now approach money matters.
- I resent the way my partner's past has made an impact on my/our family's financial situation.
- My financial relationship with my current partner is very

different from the one I had with my previous partner(s).
* My current partner resents any financial contribution to our family from my former partner.
* I feel angry that my earnings are taken into account when assessing maintenance for my partner's children.
* My partner's ex doesn't keep up with maintenance payments and that makes me feel resentful towards my stepchildren.

Your children
* My children do/don't understand the financial pressures on me.
* I feel differently about my financial responsibilities towards my birth children and my stepchildren.
* The children from my different relationships make different financial demands on me.
* I find it easy to talk to my children about money issues.
* My birth children and stepchildren have different experiences of money and wealth which causes me concern.
* My stepchildren are very manipulative about money.
* My birth children and my stepchildren have very different attitudes to money.
* I worry that I can't provide the same material benefits for my children as my former partner or other parts of our extended family.

What kinds of patterns have emerged? Is your financial lifestyle and your approach to money similar to your parents' or radically different? What kind of impact have previous relationships had on your attitude towards money? Do you treat your own children in the way you were treated? What in your experience has made it particularly easy or especially difficult to talk about money? Is there any statement that

145

you've ticked that you would like to try and change? For further exercises and detailed advice on financial planning get hold of the book *His, Hers and Theirs: A Financial Handbook for Stepfamilies.*

Closing comments

Everybody in a stepfamily can feel out of step, confused or deeply unhappy at times whether over a short or long period. Adults often know that something needs to change but do not know what or how to bring about change. Children do not have the decision-making power of adults, but they can put many pressures on the adults, and they struggle with the anxiety and fears we have talked about here - abandonment, loss of love, feelings of neglect. To deal with these issues and pressures the couple must be strong and able to support each other. This book, and the series of meetings which may accompany it, provide a beginning for identifying the nature of stepfamilies and some ideas about increasing communication skills and problem-solving. It is only a beginning, and only a few weeks out of your personal and stepfamily life. Other resources are and will be needed along the way, and perhaps one of the best that you have is other stepfamilies.

Here is a quote from a step-parent:

> *"In step-parenting your greatest ally is time."*

You have to use it well, and let it do its healing work.

Summary

There are many complexities in the law relating to families and stepfamilies. We have only touched on them. Where the answers lie outside these brief summaries, couples can approach various services, such as mediation services when visits or contact are proving difficult or need changing. The **National Stepfamily Association** has information for stepfamilies which is far more comprehensive than the points made here.

There are many aspects of stepfamily life which can cause confusion and a sense of helplessness. Information can help reduce the sense of helplessness, and help to accept what cannot be controlled.

Notes to myself on what I have learned

Resources

STEPFAMILY CLOCK
TIME AND RELATIONSHIPS

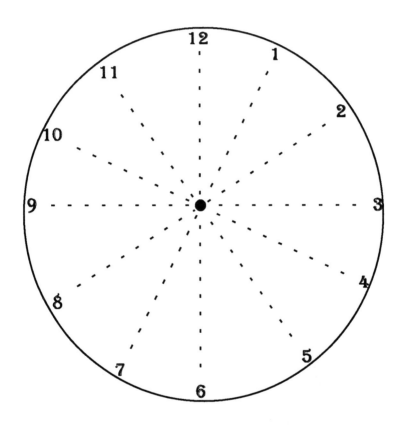

How much time do you spend doing things just for you?

How much time do you spend with your partner?

How much time do you spend as a stepfamily?

How much time do you spend with each of your children/ stepchildren?

STEPFAMILY
COAT OF ARMS

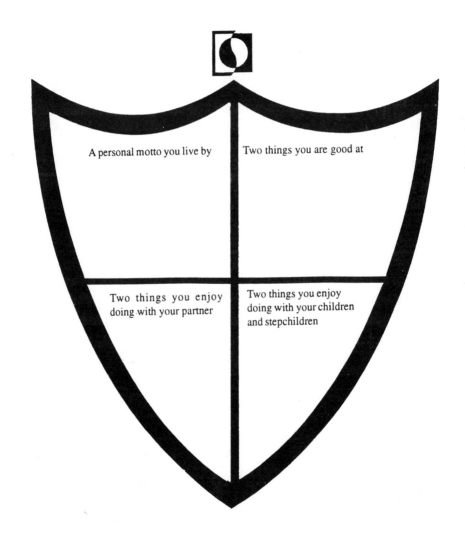

A personal motto you live by

Two things you are good at

Two things you enjoy doing with your partner

Two things you enjoy doing with your children and stepchildren

Useful Resorces

Books

A list of over 50 book specifically selected on stepfamily issues for step-parents and parents, and another list of over 60 books for children is available from the National Stepfamily Association. Some of these may be hard to obtain and some are out of print but most should be available through your library.

Particularly useful self-help books that should be in the shops are:
Step-parents, Stepchildren, Step by Step Christina IHughes (1993)
Other People's Children Suzie Hayman (1994)

Books published by the National Stepfamily Association are available by mail order.

Tapes and videos

There are a few tapes and videos on general parent issues but very little on stepfamily matters. The main providers are:

for audio tapes:
Teenagers and Stepfamilies, Teenagers and Divorce (and others), The Trust for the Study of Adolescence, 23 New Road, Brighton, East Sussex BN1 1WZ

for videos on parents separating:
Tavistock Institute of Marital Studies, Tavistock Centre, 120 Belsize Lane, London NW3 5BA

for tapes, videos and books for parent discussion groups:
Family Caring Trust Parenting Programme,
44 Rathfriland Road, Newry, Co. Down, BT34 1LD

Organisations

For informal advice and support

Exploring Parenthood
4 Ivory Place
Treadgold Street
London
W11 4BP
Tel: 0171 221 6681

Families Need Fathers
(National Admin Centre),
134 Curtain Road
London EC2A 3AR
Tel: 0171 613 5060

Gingerbread,
16-17 Clerkenwell Close
London EC1R 0AA
England Advice Line:
0171 336 8184
Wales Advice Line:
01792 648 728

Grandparents Federation,
Moot House, The Stow
Harlow, Essex CM20 3AG
Tel: 01279 444964

Home-Start UK,
2 Salisbury Road,
Leicester LE7 7QR
Tel: 01533 554988
Fax: 01533 549323

Mothers Apart From Their
Children (MATCH)
c/o BM Problems,
London WC1N 3XX

National Council For One Parent
Families
255 Kentish Town Road
London NW5 2LX
Tel: 0171 267 1361

National Stepfamily Association
3rd Floor, Chapel House
18 Hatton Place
London EC1N 8RU
Helpline: 0171 209 2464
Tel: 0171 209 2460
Fax: 0171 209 2461

One Parent Families Scotland
13 Gayfield Square
Edinburgh
EH1 3NX
Tel: 0131 556 3899

Parent Network
44-46 Caversham Road
London NW5 2DS
Tel: 0171 485 8535
Fax: 0171 267 4426

Parentline
Westbury House
57 Hart Road
Thundersley
Essex SS7 3PP
Helpline: 01268 757077
Fax: 01268 757039

Soldiers' Sailors' And Airmen's
Families Association (SSAFA)
19 Queen Elizabeth Street
London SE1 2LP
Tel: 0171 403 8783

For counselling or therapy

Asian Family Counselling
Service,
74 The Avenue, West Ealing,
London W13 8LB
Tel: 0181 997 5749

Marriage Care
23 Kensington Square,
London W8 5HN
Tel: 0171 243 1898

Institute for Family Therapy
43 New Cavendish Street
London W1M 7RG
Tel: 0171 935 1651

Jewish Marriage Council
23 Ravenshurst Avenue
London NW4 4EE
Tel: 0181 203 6311
Tel. Advice: 0181 203 6314
Helpline: 0345 581 999

London Marriage Guidance
Council
76a New Cavendish Street
Corner of Harley Street
London W1M 7LB
Tel: 0171 580 1087

National Council For The
Divorced and Separated
13 High Street, Little Shelford
Cambridgeshire CB2 5ES
Tel: 0116 270 0595

RELATE, Marriage Guidance
Herbert Gray College
Little Church Street, Rugby
Warwickshire CV21 3AP
Tel: 01788 573 241
Fax: 01788 535 007

Westminster Pastoral Foundation
23 Kensington Square
London W8 5HN
Tel: 0171 937 6956

Youth Access
Ashby House
62a Ashby Road
Loughborough
LE11 3AE
Tel: 01509 210 420

For mediation
Family Mediation Scotland
127 Rose Street, South Lane
Edinburgh EH2 4BB
Tel: 0131 220 1610

Family Mediators Association
PO Box 2028, Hove
East Sussex BN3 3HU
Tel: 01273 747 750

National Family Mediation
9 Tavistock Place
London WC1H 9SN
Tel: 0171 383 5993
Fax: 0171 383 5994

Solicitors' Family Law
Association,
PO Box 302, Orpington
Kent BR6 8QX
Tel: 01689 850 227

For legal advice
Children's Legal Centre,
The University of Essex
Wivenhoe Park
Colchester CO4 3SQ
Tel: 01206 873 820

National Association Of Citizens
Advice Bureau
Myddleton House
115-123 Pentonville Road
London, N1 9LZ
Tel: 0171 833 2181

Solicitors' Family Law
Association,
PO Box 302, Orpington
Kent BR6 8QX
Tel: 01689 850 227

For general social security, benefits and welfare advice
Child Support Agency,
24th Floor, Millbank Tower,
21-24 Millbank, London
SW1 4QU
Tel: 0171 217 4789
National Enquiry Line:
0345 133 133
Employers Enquiry Line:
0345 134 134
Child Support Literature Line:
0345 830 830

The telephone directory, Town Hall or library can direct you to your local:
Citizens Advice Bureau
Legal Advice Centre
Social Security Department

Helplines

The information below are other Helplines when the issues are more than stepfamily ones.
Reminder: Local Helplines are usually listed in the front of the Thomson Directories, and sometimes in local papers.

AIDS
National Helpline
0800 567123 - 24hrs

Alcoholics Anonymous
England   0171 352 3001
10am - 10pm Sat/Sun
9am-5pm Mon-Fri
Scotland 0141 221 9027 24hr
Wales   01646 695555 24hr
N Ireland   01232 681084
9.00am - 5pm Mon-Fri

Al-Anon Family Groups
UK and Eire   0171 403 0888

Advice, Advocacy and Representation Service for Children
0800   616101
4.00pm - 10pm Sun

Anti-Bullying Campaign
0171 378 1446
9.30am - 5pm Mon-Fri
Answerphone after hrs

Brook Advisory Centres
0171 617 8000 24hr

Beaumont Trust (help for transvestites and transexuals and their families)
0171 730 7453

Cruse (Bereavement Care)
0181 332 7227
(9.30am-5pm, Mon-Fri)

Children's Legal Centre
01206   873820
2.00pm-5pm Mon - Fri

The Compassionate Friends (for parents whose child of any age has died)
0117 9539639
9.30am - 5pm Mon-Fri

Childwatch (abuse)
01482   585214
10.00am-10pm - Mon-Thurs

Childline
0800 1111

Cot Death Helpline
(Foundation for the Study of Infant Deaths)
0171 235 1721

Exploring Parenthood
Parents advice line
0171 221 6681

Enuresis (bed-wetting)
(Resource/info centre)
0117 9264920
9.30am - 5.30pm- Mon-Fri

Families Need Fathers (non
custodial/residential parents)
0181 886 0970
0171 613 5060

Family Mediators Association
0181 954 6383

Felag (Families and Friends of
Lesbians and Gays)
0161 628 76 21
0116 2708331 Leicester
9.00am - 9pm

Gingerbread
England   0171 336 8183
11.00pm-2pm   Mon-Fri
Scotland   0141 353 0953
N. Ireland   01232 234568
Wales   01792 648728

Grandparents Federation
01279 437145

Help the Aged
0800 289404
10.00am - 4pm - Mon-Fri

Incest Crisis
0181 890 4732

Kidscape (bullying/getting lost,
threat of abuse by known adults)
0171 730 3300
9.30am - 5pm Mon - Wed

Life (pregnancy/abortion
counselling)
01926 311511
9.00am - 9pm - Mon-Sun

Meet-a-Mum (M.A.M.A)
0181 656 7378
3.30am - 11 pm - Mon-Fri
11.00am - 8 pm - Sat/Sun

Missing Persons Bureau
0181 392 2000
24hrs - Mon-Sun

Mediation UK
01272 241234 (Bristol)

Narcotics Anonymous
0171 498 9005
10.00am-8pm - Mon-Sun

National Family Mediation
0171 383 5993

National Stepfamily Assoc.
0171 209 2464
2.00pm - 5.00pm
7.00pm - 10.00pm Mon-Fri

Network '81 (parents of children
with special educ. needs)
01279 647415
1.00pm - 4 pm - Mon-Fri

NSPCC (abused children and
their families)
0800 800 500 24hrs

Norcap (Nat. Org. for
Counselling Adoptees and their
Parents)
01865 750554
10.00-4 pm Mon-Wed-Fri

NCH Careline
0181 514 1177

National Debtline
0121 359 8501

Central Parentline
01268 757077
9.00am -6pm Mon-Fri
10.00am-2pm Sat,
after hrs numbers supplied on
answerphone.

Local Parentline Groups
Altrincham   0161 9414011
Belfast   01232 238800
Convey Island   01268 511151
Croydon   0181 668 4805
Doncaster   01302 328 668
Dublin   003531 8733500
Herts   0171 327541
L'Derry   01504 266663
Milton Keynes   01908 317868
Newbury   01635 46217
Newcastle   0191 281 4881
Nottingham   0115 9402405
Nuneaton   01203 374120
Oxford   01865 726600
Peterborough   01733 312 457
Redditch   01527 60266
Sheffield   0114 2726575
Shropshire   01952 641370
Southampton   01703 694013
Suffolk   01449 677500
Surrey   0306 880755
Uttlesford   01799 520000

Parents at Work (formerly
Working Mothers Association)
0171 700 5771
9.00am-1pm 2.00pm-4pm
Tues, Thurs, Fri

Post-Adoption Centre (step-
parents adoptions)
0171 284 0555

Pre-Learning Alliance
0171 837 5513
10.00am-5 Mon-Fri

Rape Crisis Centre
0171 837 1600
Scotland 0131 556 9437

Refuge (domestic violence)
0181 995 4430 24hrs

Samaritans Phone Book/Ask
Oper. to put you through
01753 532713 (Slough)

SANDS (Stillborn and Neonatal
Deaths)
0171 436 5881

Shelter (homelessness)
Emerg. London Nightline
0800 446441
6.00pm - 9pm Mon-Fri
24hrs Sat-Sun
answerphone during the day
Scotland   0131 313 150
9.30am - 5.30pm answerphone

Survivors of Sexual Abuse
0181 890 4732
24hrs answerphone

Spastics Society (Now Scope)
0800 626216
11-9 pm Mon-Fri
2pm-6pm Sat-Sun

Victim Support Schemes
Ask local police for nearest
group
National Ass. 0116 2558763

Women's Aid Refuges
0117 9633542

Women Against Rape
0171 700 5771
and answerphone

Working Mothers Parents at
Work
  0171 700 5771
  9-1 am 2-4 pm Tues, Thurs, Fri

Women's Aid Federation
  England 0117 9 633542
  Scotland 0131 221 0401
  10am -1pm Mon-Fri
  answerphone after hrs

OTHERS

Advisory Centre for Education
(ACE)
  0171 354 8321
  2-5 Mon-Fri

**Asian Family Counselling
Service**
  0181 997 5749

Law Centres Federation
  0171 387 8570

Books Available from STEPFAMILY

Another Step: Weddings in Stepfamilies *Kathleen Cox (1995)* £4.00 (£3.40)*

Stepfathering *Stephen Kaye (1995)* £4.00 (£3.40)*

His, Hers, Theirs; A Financial Handbook for Stepfamilies. *Tobe Aleksander (1995)* £6.50 (£5.50)*

A Baby of Our Own, A new baby in a stepfamily *Erica De'Ath (1993) Endorsed by the Health Visitors Association.* £4.00 (£3.40)*

Parenting Threads: Caring for Children When Couples Part *(Editors) Erica De'Ath & Dee Slater (1992)* £4.00 (£3.40)*

* members prices

Please send me details of

STEPFAMILY membership
other publications - leaflets and books
how to become a volunteer telephone counsellor
more information on donating to STEPFAMILY

Name ....

Address ....

.... Postcode ....

Please return this form to:
STEPFAMILY, 3rd Floor, Chapel House, 18 Hatton Place
London EC1N 8RU tel 0171 209 2460

Registered Charity No. 1005351   Company No. 2552166

STEPFAMILY is the only national organisation providing support, advice and information for all members of stepfamilies and those who work with them. We have local contacts and groups in Northern Ireland, Scotland, Wales and England. We are also helping stepfamilies to set up their own organisation in Sweden, Belguim, Denmark and Australia.

☯

STEPFAMILY offers a wide range of services to members:

☯

confidential telephone counselling

☯

2 newsletters
STEPFAMILY for adults
STEPLADDER for children

☯

local support groups

☯

information packs, books and leaflets

☯

conferences, seminars and training workshops

Founder Elizabeth Hodder
Company Limited by guarantee 2552166
Charity Registration No. 1005351